"Bill and Pam Farrel have used their delightful humor, practical knowledge, and biblical truth to help me and countless others understand and appreciate the differences between men and women. Their very real approach has improved my marriage tremendously, and I know that all they have to say about the challenges of sustaining a successful marriage will enrich yours as well."

Stormie Omartian
author of *The Power of a Praying Wife*

"If anyone should be writing a book about marriage it should be the Farrels. Experience is always better than supposition. These two practice what they preach—thus their effectiveness in ministering to others. *The 10 Best Decisions a Couple Can Make* is truly a practical guide to the art of staying in love and finishing the journey well as a couple. Take it from a couple who knows."

Michelle McKinney Hammond
author of *The Power of Being a Woman*

"Why settle for a run-down marriage when you can create something beautiful? *The 10 Best Decisions a Couple Can Make* offers insights and wisdom to help you move your marriage from tenement to tasteful villa. Enjoy!"

Jerry and Patti MacGregor
authors of *Family Times* and
The Prayers of the Presidents

"Every marriage is a work in progress, and wise couples will realize that an occasional relationship remodeling job is necessary to stay in love for a lifetime. Bill and Pam Farrel understand the upkeep needed to care for a relationship in the same way upkeep is needed to maintain a home. You'll laugh, you'll cry, and you'll identify with their honesty about the challenges and the benefits of love for a lifetime!"

Jill Savage
executive director of Hearts at Home
author of *Is There Really Sex After Kids?*

"Pam and Bill believe marriages can last a lifetime—and so can love! A loveless marriage is a terrible thing to live with—and it doesn't have to be! This book is written with humor and sincerity from the vantage point of 'silver anniversary' status! If you have lost your first love, learn how to renew your relationship and reverse the trend. Highly recommended."

Jill Briscoe
r of *God's Front Door*

D0368272

"Whether you have been married for many years or are newlyweds, Bill and Pam will break down the secrets to lifelong love into bite-sized, easy-to-apply pieces. Through their humor, vulnerability, and easy-to-apply biblical and prayer principles, you will experience a closer walk with God and happiness in your marriage relationship. Now *that's* a win-win situation!"

Fern Nichols
founder of Moms in Touch International
author of *Every Child Needs a Praying Mom*

"Marriage is indeed worth the investment! This book is a great place to start. Bill and Pam deliver sound and practical advice for anyone wanting to freshen up a good marriage or even do a complete makeover."

H. Dale Burke
author of *Different by Design*
and *Less Is More Leadership*

"Pam and Bill Farrel live what they teach. They are a committed couple, caring parents, and ongoing faithful friends. Their marriage ministry is *real*. They talk to people about the ups and downs of marriage and then use examples from their own 25-year relationship, which gives their words credibility and integrity."

Karen O'Connor
author of *Getting Old Ain't for Wimps*

"Practical, biblical, humorous, and real—Bill and Pam will fill your hearts with the tools to build lasting marital love. A must read."

Claudia and **David Arp**
authors of the 10 Great Dates
series and *No Time for Sex*

"Bill and Pam have done it again! They are awesome communicators about marriage. This book will help fix and strengthen marriages with its clear, honest, and humorous approach! Even your husband will want to read it—no matter whether he's like Bob Vila or Tim the Tool Man Taylor."

Kathy Collard Miller
author of *Partly Cloudy with Scattered Worries*

"All married couples—young and seasoned—will benefit greatly from this insightful new book that lays a solid foundation for making love last a lifetime."

Janet Holm McHenry
author of *Prayer Changes Teens:
How to Parent from Your Knees*

The 10 Best Decisions a Couple Can Make

Bill & Pam Farrel

HARVEST HOUSE PUBLISHERS

EUGENE, OREGON

Cover by Left Coast Design, Portland, Oregon

Cover photo © Jim Erickson / Workbookstock

Bill Farrel: Published in association with the literary agency of Alive Communications, Inc., 7680 Goddard Street, Ste #200, Colorado Springs, CO 80920.

Pam Farrel: Published in association with the literary agency of Alive Communications, Inc., 7680 Goddard Street, Ste #200, Colorado Springs, CO 80920.

THE 10 BEST DECISIONS A COUPLE CAN MAKE
Copyright © 2005 by Bill and Pam Farrel
Published by Harvest House Publishers
Eugene, Oregon 97402
www.harvesthousepublishers.com

Previously published as Every Marriage Is a Fixer-Upper

Library of Congress Cataloging-in-Publication Data
    Farrel, Bill, 1959-
    [Every marriage is a fixer-upper]
    The 10 best decisions a couple can make / Bill and Pam Farrel.
        p. cm.
    Originally published: Every marriage is a fixer-upper. Eugene, Or. : Harvest House, c2005.
    ISBN-13: 978-0-7369-2182-4
    ISBN-10: 0-7369-2182-6
    1. Marriage—Religious aspects—Christianity. 2. Interpersonal communication—Religious aspects—Christianity. I. Farrel, Pam, 1959- II. Title. III. Title: Ten best decisions a couple can make.
    BT835.F37 2007
    248.8'44—dc22
                                                                            2007030585

To our first granddaughter, Eden:

May your wise decisions make your parents
as proud of you as we are of them.

Love and prayers,

Papa So-Cal and *Nana Go-Go*

Contents

1

Decide to Build a Love That Lasts

*Here's to marriage, that happy estate that
resembles a pair of scissors: So joined that they cannot
be separated, often moving in opposite directions,
yet punishing anyone who comes between them.*

—SYDNEY SMITH

How would a real estate agent describe your marriage? *Rare find! Ideal! Outstanding and sharp! Beautiful and elegant! Mint condition! Fabulous!* Most marriages would get a more realistic description: *Remodeled charmer. Solid foundation but needs some TLC. Great curb appeal but interior needs a major remodel. Good neighborhood—a cozy fixer-upper!*

The television listings are filled with home-improvement shows, including *Trading Spaces, Extreme Makeover: Home Edition, Merge,* and *While You Were Out,* just to name a few. The long list of fix-it shows includes *This Old House, Bob Vila's Home Again,* and *Designing for the Sexes.* These shows demonstrate effective techniques and strategies for making any dwelling a better place to call home. In the same way, your marriage needs a strategy for staying in good shape.

Just as the walls don't paint themselves, the grass won't mow itself, and the dishes won't wash themselves, a marriage doesn't magically become strong and beautiful on its own. Creating a beautiful home requires a good set of plans, a competent contractor, able craftsmen, and gifted decorators.

Everything worthwhile is worth investing in. Homes that receive consistent tender loving care are appraised at a higher value. In the same way, every marriage given consistent love and attention will become a work of art, a sanctuary of love, and a haven of hope.

Think of this book as a set of plans for building a long-lasting love. Your first step is to decide to build a love that lasts. Decide that you want to discover what makes love last for a lifetime. Decide to look for a good set of plans for building a love and a life. We want to take a humorous and practical look at marriage and provide everyday tools for the couple who wants to do a little work around the house and create a home you both want to come home to—a home built with love.

Lessons from the Contractor

As of the writing of this book, we have been the proud owners of three homes. They have all been projects, and they have helped us learn some of the most important lessons in our relationship.

We thought our first home was the most awesome thing we had ever seen. It was built in the 1950s, but it looked like a shiny new diamond to us. The bright yellow and orange wallpaper in the kitchen looked hideous, but we thought, *This is not a problem. We'll just put up new wallpaper.* The green shag carpet throughout the house was nauseating, but we thought, *This is not a problem. We'll just rip it up and refinish the hardwood floors.* We had heard that the house had termites, but we thought, *This is not a problem. The house has just been fumigated, so all the termites are dead.*

Looking back, we realize this was relationship lesson number one. We all go into our marriages thinking, *This is not a problem. We'll just work it all out because we're in love.* This idealism is probably necessary because if we knew everything that is involved in building an intimate relationship, we would conclude it is impossible and run the other way. But we seem to have a marvelous magnet in our hearts that convinces us we desperately need each other.

Actually, every marriage has bugs, viruses, challenges, inconsistencies, and shortcomings. As Dr. Harry Ironside is famous for saying,

"Where there is light, there is bugs." Successful married couples learn to live with their eyes wide open to the challenges and assume they will have to remodel their relationship on a regular basis to counteract the natural process of decay.

What Is This?

And so with youthful enthusiasm we began our adventure. With wide eyes and expectant hearts we launched into fixing up our "new" home. We started by tearing down the hideous wallpaper in the kitchen. Attached to the kitchen was a breakfast nook with a bay window with wood frames, and the nook was accented with a wooden wainscot. The wainscot was not original, so we decided to remove it as we were remodeling the kitchen.

As I (Bill) was enthusiastically taking the wood paneling off the wall, one of the windowsills came with it! The rotten piece of wood dropped to the floor. It had obviously been the home of termites for a long time. A cavernous network of tunnels ran through the wood. Parts of the sill were nothing more than a paper-thin facade. I'm not sure, but I think I heard the house laughing at me. With the sill on the floor, I could clearly see the bottom of the window frame. What I saw there was amazing. Dead termites were stacked on one another. The bottom half of the frame was almost totally eaten up. Some fat termites must have been running around that neighborhood! I remember thinking, *What have I done?* We knew about the termites, but no one told us we were buying the Home Town Buffet for bugs!

Lesson number two: Every couple goes through a period where they wonder, *What have we gotten ourselves into?* No one could possibly anticipate all that is involved in an intimate relationship, so surprises are inevitable. I remember my first big surprise. Pam and I were quietly sitting in our living room during our first year of marriage. I was thinking to myself, *This is awesome. She is beautiful, sex is great, and we're young and having a lot of fun together.* Then it happened. I said something that pushed some button in Pam.

She abruptly stood up and exclaimed, "You don't love me

anymore!" Then she ran to our bedroom, slammed the door, and sprawled herself across the bed. When I walked in, she was sobbing violently. I knew our marriage would hold some challenges, but no one ever told me about this!

I have since learned that one of the best things I can do for Pam is to help her feel secure. She needs to know that she is important and valued. I know that now, but I didn't then. That day she ran into our room, I wondered who this person was and where she had taken my wife.

I Have a Dream!

Back to the house. I had to hire a contractor to remake the window frame because matching windows were no longer available. With his expert help, we repaired the window and continued on with the kitchen.

The old wallpaper had to come off because we decided to paint. For some reason, we thought that paint would look better and be easier to clean. Covering the wall with new paper would have been easier, but *we had a dream.*

The wallpaper was stubborn, so we had to rent a steamer. Nobody told me that a steamer is like a boiling serpent looking for someone to attack. It sputtered. It clogged. It refused to work. It was just plain stubborn. I could have stopped early in the process and put up wallpaper, but *we had a dream.* So I committed to "fix" the steamer. In the process, I sprayed myself in the face with steam. It scared me and made me more determined at the same time. Fortunately, all I received was an unwanted sunburn for my efforts! At that point, I probably should have said to Pam, "We need to give up this plan and wallpaper the kitchen." But *we had a dream!* I am proud to say that after much travail, the kitchen was beautifully painted with contrasting trim on the wood windows.

Lesson number three: At times the only thing that keeps a couple going is *the dream.* Intimate relationships are very influential on our hearts. They are filled with hopes and dreams and disappointments.

The relationship begins with the feeling that it will be magical and fulfilling. The dream gets interrupted by the real needs of the individuals involved. A lifetime of marriage is filled with disappointments, setbacks, misunderstandings, times of great responsibility, financial decisions, and many other challenges. No man ever said to a young woman, "Will you marry me so we can load up on bills and work hard the rest of our lives to pay them off?" But when reality hits, a couple can endure some boring, stressful, and painful times because of the dream: We can rediscover our love over and over again. A couple with this dream will work together to build a place where their relationship works. The dream gets them through the unexpected.

After we finished remodeling the kitchen, the dream expanded. As we grew accustomed to our new home, we entertained a foolish thought: *This is not enough.* Lesson number four: Something in the hearts of men and women easily becomes discontent. We have cars, but they aren't nice enough. We have computers, but they aren't fast enough. We have homes, but they aren't big enough. We have relationships, but they aren't good enough.

We get married to the person of our dreams but grow discontent because we forget the dream in the light of reality. What was beautiful in the night fades in the daylight. A joke we read puts it this way: "Did you ever notice that when you fall in love, you sink into his arms, but after the wedding, your arms are in his sink?" In every relationship, the dream must withstand the realities of everyday life.

The "not good enough" bug bit us, and we decided we needed to add a master bathroom to our house. The project seemed simple as we talked about it. We would just move the front door and then simply turn the entryway into a bathroom. What we thought would take about a month to finish took almost five times that long. I would love to tell you that Pam was very proud of me and said, "Wow, honey, I appreciate your perseverance. Even though this is taking longer than you thought, I am amazed at the way you're sticking to the task. By the way, you look really sexy in dirty construction clothes!"

Instead, the comments degraded from "I'm so excited!" to "How long did you say this was going to take? Don't you think you should get someone else to finish this? I'm beginning to think you like working on the house better than spending time with me."

Even though hiring a contractor would probably have been a good idea, my ego winced. My thoughts had originally been noble: *I'm going to do this for my new wife.* But as time went on, my thoughts turned sour. *I'll show her. I can't believe she doesn't think I can do this! Why is she complaining? This was her idea!* I had lost sight of the dream.

Survived Once—Do It Again!

Our second house is a very different story. With great expectation and enthusiasm we moved to San Diego County to pastor a church. We assumed we could sell the home we remodeled and buy a home in Southern California. During the first three months we were in San Diego, however, the average house rose $40,000 in value, and we were priced right out of the market.

I did not want to build a house. I had worked as an architectural draftsman for years before becoming a pastor. I helped many people design custom homes for their families, and as I watched these families go through the process of building their homes, I concluded *I will never do this!* Somehow, God must not have heard me correctly.

The people of the church were incredibly gracious. A plumber told me, "If you want to build a house, I'll donate my time to put in the plumbing." I replied, "Thanks for the offer, but we're not going to build a house."

An electrician told me, "If you want to build a house, I'll donate my time to install the wiring." Again I said, "Thanks for the offer, but we're not going to build a house."

A heating and air conditioning contractor told me, "If you want to build a house, I'll donate my time to install the heating system." I repeated, "Thanks for the offer, but we're not going to build a house."

A roofer told me, "If you want to build a house, I'll donate my time to install the roofing." Still I said, "Thanks for the offer, but we're not going to build a house."

I began to think a conspiracy was going on. I didn't want to do this, but God was inspiring people to be incredibly generous. Generosity is a great trait, but it can be irritating when you have an attitude! With the hope that He wouldn't come through, I made a deal with God. I told Him, *I know a man who is a construction supervisor. He's only working four days a week right now. If he approaches me, tells me I should build, and offers to walk me through the whole process, I will build. But he has to approach me!*

You can probably figure out what happened next. This friend walked up to me and said, "Hey, Bill, I think you should build a home. I'm only working four days a week right now, and I'm willing to walk you through the whole process."

My mouth fell open so fast, I think I bruised my chin on the floor. I wanted to say, "Thanks for the offer, but we're not going to build a house." What I said instead was...nothing. I was so dumbfounded that I couldn't say a thing. I finally squeaked out, "I'll get back to you."

Based on this interaction, I found property, drew up plans for our home, and acquired a permit. The week I received the permit, my friend was honored with the job of his dreams. It took advantage of all of his gifts and blessed him with a large salary increase. It also required six days a week and long hours. As a result, he wasn't able to walk us through the process of building our home. *I needed a miracle!*

Lesson number five: All great relationships start when people choose to trust God. We are all imperfect people trying to love other imperfect people in an imperfect world. Therefore, we all have perfectly imperfect marriages. The greatest moment of your marriage is when you realize you don't have all the answers, when in reckless abandon you throw your hands up in the air and say to God, *Okay, we'll do it Your way! Lead on.*

That's exactly what happened with the house. I'll never forget the Friday morning I was standing on my newly poured foundation. The framers were to arrive the next day, and my job was to get everything ready for them. I had never done this before. I had committed to this because someone with experience was willing to walk me through. Now that man was not available, and I was standing on my cement, asking God for wisdom and any help He could send my way.

My new neighbor happened to have a day off from work that day. He also happened to have experience preparing job sites for a framing company. He volunteered about four hours to show me how to mark the studs so the workers could stay busy. That was just one of many stories.

One day, I was digging footings for the front and back patios. When I started digging, I said to God, *I sure could use a small jackhammer.* Within an hour a plumber friend of mine came by and told me, "As I was leaving this morning, I got this nudging from the Lord that maybe you needed a jackhammer, so I put it in my truck. Do you need it today?"

Another day, I met a young man who had just been discharged from the Marines. He wanted to stay in San Marcos and be a part of our church because he had recently asked Christ into his life. We had a travel trailer on our property, so I had him live in the trailer and trade work for rent. Not only did he prove to be a huge help in getting work done, but I was able to train him in the basics of Christianity while we worked. We didn't have time to stop and do any lessons, so we did them as we worked. Some of my greatest memories of building the house include writing those discipleship lessons on the wood under the carpet and under the paint. Nobody will ever see them, but they helped change the life of a young man. As we have raised our kids in the same house, I am reminded that people will never see the lessons written on the hearts of our kids, but the results will be lifelong.

To make matters even more interesting, I (Pam) was pregnant, and we were racing the stork to get the house done before the baby came. The whole event became a town spectacle, and a local newspaper even featured us in an article. People were taking bets on whether we'd get in before the baby arrived. Even our two older sons, Brock, then six, and Zach, then four, were part of the crew. Zach was one of Bill's best coworkers, and together they sided half the house in one day. (Actually, they only sided the bottom half so Zach could reach to nail the boards!)

We endured a pretty strenuous 18-month process from conception (of the house, not the baby!) to our move-in day—two weeks after Caleb arrived. The actual building time was about the same as the pregnancy. During this nine months, Bill was pastoring full-time and building full-time, so he was getting very little sleep. My job was running around town, taking care of the kids, and providing on-site meals. I ran the phone lines, tied steel rebar for the foundation, hammered together walls, and helped insulate, finish wallboard, and clean up each day. I have a renewed appreciation for what the homestead women went through on their trek west!

The two days before Caleb was born, Bill stayed up 48 hours straight while the driveway was being poured and the concrete was setting. We thought we had a shot at bringing the baby home to our new house, so he burned the candle at both ends. I went to the hospital for a scheduled C-section on August 3 at six a.m., and Bill, the amazing dutiful husband, was by my side all the way. However, when I came out of recovery, I looked better than Bill did!

The first day after a C-section, Mom is supposed to stay flat in bed. But in the middle of the night after feeding Caleb, I tried to wake Bill, who had crashed in an uncomfortable folding chair. When I couldn't wake him, I attempted to sit up enough to place Caleb in his clear bassinet.

Accomplishing this was no small feat, but with prayer, determination, and mothering instincts, I set Caleb safely in his bed. In the process, my IV got tangled and was pulled out of my hand. Blood began to spray everywhere. I pushed the nurse's button and yelled for Bill. Bill was in such poor shape that I couldn't wake him. I was up and had walked partway to the center station before a nurse came to help me. Bill never moved an inch, deep in REM sleep!

Even the nurse noticed and said, "Deep sleeper, huh?"

I explained all that Bill had done for our family and me the past few months, and she smiled in approval. I looked over at my sleeping prince charming, and a rush of love overwhelmed me. I knew regardless of what life threw our way, we'd find a way to stay in love for a lifetime. I had married a real keeper!

Upkeep for the Keeper

When our house was finally completed, I (Bill) was exhausted. All I wanted was to go to work, come home, eat, and sleep. I figured I had earned the right to live at a slow pace for at least a year. But I have a family! Our three boys are just that—boys—and that means things in our home are often broken.

In order to obtain the final permit to move into our house, I had to install a sprinkler system and groundcover on the hill in my backyard. About two months after we had moved in, I pulled into the driveway after a day at work, when suddenly something flew over the windshield of my car. As I got out of the car, I looked in the backyard and saw my two older boys and one of their friends with baseball bats in their hands, practicing their golf swings on my sprinkler heads! I couldn't believe what I was seeing. I felt as if I were in a bad dream I couldn't escape from. I told the boys' friend to go home immediately. He dropped the bat and ran like a gazelle. I then said to my boys, "You'd better get in the house before I do something we all regret."

I wandered around the house for the next hour in a disillusioned stupor. I found myself expecting my four- and six-year-old sons to possess the maturity of adults. *What were they thinking? Don't they realize how hard this is on me? Don't they appreciate the year of hard work I have just put in? I bet they did this just to make me mad!* As I walked around the house, I forced myself to pray one of my most profound prayers: *Jesus, I would rather have kids than sprinklers.* I had to repeat this prayer over and over again because I didn't really mean it at first. But after about an hour, I finally convinced myself that it was true.

Ever since that day, a question has haunted me: Why does life require so much maintenance? Lesson number six: Fixed things won't stay fixed. Weeds grow faster than everything else. Relationships deteriorate unless you nurture them. In other words, remodeling is a way of life.

We bought home number three because Dr. David Jeremiah offered Bill a wonderful position on the staff of Shadow Mountain Church. The new ministry position was a dream, but the 60-minute commute in Southern California traffic was a nightmare. Right away, we prayed that God would give us a home a few minutes from the church and the high school where Caleb, our youngest son, attended.

Our real estate agent, Cynthia, found a home on a hillside with a gorgeous view three minutes away from work and school, but it seemed a little unusual. The owner was a machinist, and his "shop" was 800 square feet and sat next to the home. The home was built over a seven-car garage, where he restored antique cars. We only had two cars (three if you count the 20-year-old VW our son was trying to get running again). I loved the cabin feel of the upstairs, but Bill never seemed to make it up there. Every time we visited the home to decide whether to buy it, Bill stood downstairs, pondering the enormity of the garage. Finally, a little perplexed by this behavior, I marched downstairs and said, "Bill, you don't need a seven-car garage!"

Then my very wise husband smiled his broad, beautiful grin, the one that made me first fall in love with him, and said, "Pam, picture this. Two-car garage, three offices, and a guest room suite. And the shop can hold all the books and products as our ministry grows!"

He was brilliant! He could see what I had missed—the amazing potential for a bright future housed in the shell of that garage. And that's the attitude we hope you two embrace as you read this book. Don't look at the problems, look at the potential of your love!

A Real-Life Toolbox

We have always lived by the motto "knowledge isn't a skill until it is practical." To make this book as practical as possible, we've enlisted the help of couples who have a proven track record. We asked couples who describe their marriage as happy and strong and have been married more than 20 years to put in their two cents. Throughout this book you'll find their stories and their words of wisdom.

In past centuries, young men apprenticed under master craftsmen to learn trades such as ironwork, brick masonry, and carpentry. We hope this book will be an apprentice program for your love whether you have been married a few days or more than 30 years. Each chapter will present practical skills to help you keep your marriage in top shape.

Just as a craftsman learns his trade from a master mentor craftsman, we have discovered it is helpful to have marriage mentors. During the weeks you are reading this book together, we encourage you to find a couple you admire and ask if they will meet you once a week and discuss the key concepts in each chapter. If you are currently happily married, we challenge you to become a mentor couple to a newlywed couple or a struggling couple and pass on the wealth of wisdom you have accumulated. In giving away the secrets of love, you will gain a new fresh appreciation of the love you have built together. Mentor Moment questions are included at the end of this book.

Finally, couples that have been happily married have a friendship circle around them of other couples that believe in love that lasts. This book is a great resource for small groups, so gather a few friends and use the small-group questions in the back to form a safety net for your love.

We are all in process. We are all building, remodeling, "fixin' up" our love. Our goal is to make bad marriages good and good marriages better. We have organized our thoughts around a favorite Scripture passage used in most weddings. We have chosen this set of verses because they form a strong foundation upon which all healthy relationships can be built. See if you recognize the passage:

> Love is patient, love is kind. It does not envy, it does not boast, it is not proud. It is not rude, it is not self-seeking, it is not easily angered, it keeps no record of wrongs. Love does not delight in evil but rejoices with the truth. It always protects, always trusts, always hopes, always perseveres. Love never fails...And now these three remain: faith, hope and love. But the greatest of these is love (1 Corinthians 13:4-8,13).

When a Man Enters a Home Improvement Store...

His heart rate increases.

Endorphins flood his bloodstream.

He forgets why he entered the store.

His eyes move from right to left, trying to decide where to start.

He wanders toward the tools to see what is new.

He dreams of everything he could do with a new cordless drill.

He checks out the new fencing material.

On the way to the fence materials, he notices the new ladders and compares them to the one he already owns.

He remembers that he came for lightbulbs.

On the way to the lighting section, he stops at the tools again to check out the tool belts. He wonders if he looks sexy to his wife with his tool belt on. He asks himself, *If I bought a new tool belt, would our sex life improve?* He can't figure out the answer, so he heads for the lightbulbs.

On the way to the lightbulbs, he notices the lawn mowers. He asks himself, *Do we need a riding lawn mower? If we did, which one would I want?*

He wanders down the lawn-care aisle to see what is new.

He checks out the chain saws. He doesn't need one, but he feels more like a man standing next to them.

He wonders how long he has been in the store.

He pulls the note out of his pocket to remind himself why he came to the store.

He finds the lightbulb aisle and picks up the lightbulbs.

He realizes his wife is probably wondering what happened to him.

On the way to the checkout stand, he stops at the tools again and checks out the new tape measures. He knows they don't cost very much, so he decides to get a new one.

He continues to the checkout line.

He buys the bulbs but decides at the last minute not to get the tape measure.

He gets in the car to drive home and says to himself, *I wish my wife could have been here to see all this great stuff.*

When a Woman Enters a Home Improvement Store...

She checks her list to remind herself she needs lightbulbs.

She stops at the information center and asks where the right aisle is.

On her way to the lights, she notices a lot of men in the tool section.

She asks the man in the light aisle which lights would be best for her lamp.

She puts the lightbulbs in her basket.

She heads for the checkout stand.

She wonders why three men are standing in front of the chain saws.

She buys the lightbulbs and notices that the lady at the checkout stand has the same name as her sister. She has a five-minute conversation with her because no one else is in line. She finds out the names of her two kids, where she graduated from high school, and where she will be going on vacation next summer.

She gets in the car to drive home and wonders if she just met a new friend.

2

Decide to Be Positive

Love is patient.

Do not argue with a spouse who is packing your parachute.

It looked and sounded like such a great idea! The women's magazine made the recipe look absolutely tantalizing and mouthwatering. The directions seemed so easy—I (Pam) couldn't possibly fail. Admittedly, I would definitely never call myself a chef. In fact, I would barely call myself a short-order cook. To be honest, the only reason I got higher than a C in home economics was that I had the people skills to schmooze, and I used the Tom Sawyer "white picket fence" trick. I definitely didn't learn how to cook, but I made a number of friends who knew how to cook.

I felt a lot of pressure, though, because my grandmother was a fantastic cook. She won awards for cooking at the local fair every year. People went out of their way to get a taste of her homemade biscuits. I, however, missed out on that Betty Crocker gene. When I make biscuits, people just get out of the way! But when I was a new bride, I felt a moral obligation to become the next Julia Childs. That's why I was thumbing through my women's magazines, looking for a way to completely impress my new husband. Pheasant Under Glass was just too intriguing to resist. It was fancy. It was pretty. And it sounded very refined.

I had the entire day off to develop my creation. Bill and my brother, Bret, who was staying with us at the time to relocate to our community, were at work. This meant I could take my time and make it perfect! I would have an impressive Pheasant Under Glass dinner by candlelight. Bill would be so amazed by my newfound culinary talent that he would definitely want to enjoy a romantic evening. I'd just give my brother a ticket to the movies or something to get him out of the house so Bill and I could be alone together. This dish was going to fan the flame of our love!

I thought for a moment. *What should I serve with such a sultry dish? Could I make some ordinary things seems extraordinary? Would I also have the time to bake a chocolate cake and call it Fantastic Foreplay?* Cake seemed too tame for a Pheasant Under Glass. The main dish cried for something more like Cherries Jubilee or Baked Alaska. Something with flames. In our small apartment, however, I wasn't sure I could create that same effect.

A year before, while celebrating our anniversary at a restaurant, we ordered Cherries Jubilee, and our chef prepared it at our table. He had peeled an orange so the rind looked a lot like a spiraling Slinky toy. He poured the liquor down the rind and lit it with a match. The flame spiraled down over the peel as the luscious orange juices flowed into the pan of warm cherry topping. It was magical! Brilliant! A work of art! For a brief moment, I was convinced I could replicate this feat in my own house. Then, just as instantly, I remembered the grade I should have received in home economics. I decided to not risk burning the apartment complex down. No, I should just focus all my energy and complete attention on the upscale main course.

Off I went to the grocery store. I excitedly gathered the unique ingredients—Knox unflavored gelatin, bouillon, vegetables. I looked for pheasant, but it wasn't available. I reasoned, *Everything tastes like chicken, so I guess chicken will have to do.* I picked up a whole chicken and headed to the checkout counter.

Once home, I tried to carefully follow all the instructions. I remember taking a long time because I had to boil the chicken, wait for it to cool, debone it, and then create skinny strips that would go under the "glass." I measured and I arranged. I got distracted in a TV talk show while I waited between steps. I had to do a lot of stuff that I had never done before, like make unflavored gelatin and cook with bouillon cubes. (The only gelatin we ever had growing up was lime green Jell-O with pineapple chunks and little white mini marshmallows. We had it every holiday. When Mom was really feeling festive, she'd put it in a Tupperware Jell-O mold with a little Christmas tree shape on top. I had once tried making this green Jell-O on my own, but I didn't know I was supposed to run the mold under cold water at just the right time. My Christmas tree fell out of the mold in little green Jell-O chunks.)

I arranged all the chicken strips and veggies. I poured the "glass" gelatin concoction over the chicken in the magical tin mold pan. I felt so pleased with myself that I went for a swim in the apartment complex pool. I toweled off and reclined on the chaise lounge and thought, *I feel so rich, so divine. This must be how all those women in the evening soaps feel as they lounge around waiting for their man to get home from his million-dollar producing career in the downtown high-rise office complex. This will definitely lead to an exciting evening.*

But Bill was coming home from working in the oil fields. We were struggling students, doing any kind of work to pay the rent and school bills. I had two part-time jobs. We drove a blue Vega with a green liftgate. The topic more likely on Bill's mind was how to save money to get to grad school. We certainly had no servants, no maids, no high-rise buildings in which we worked—but I did have this apartment complex pool in 110-degree Bakersfield heat and Hank Williams playing on an old radio. What more could a girl want?

In all my daydreaming about being rich, I totally forgot about serving anything with the Pheasant (I mean, chicken) Under Glass. I had no fruit, no dessert, and no bread. The rest of the meal hadn't even crossed my mind because Chicken Under Glass was the magic ticket item. Who needs to continue working in the kitchen when she has a love potion cooling in the refrigerator?

The guys came in from work. They'd had a long hot day in the oil fields and they were starved. My brother asked first, "So Sis, what's for dinner?"

"It's a surprise!"

"A surprise, huh, honey? Must be good!" Bill quipped as I heard his stomach growl.

"Oh, it will be. The table is all set—honey, will you go ahead and light the candles?"

Bill readily accommodated my request.

"Okay, are you ready?"

"Sure are!" they both said, picking up their forks.

I pulled the tray out of the refrigerator. The chicken mold was garnished, and I admired my creation. I set it in the center of the table.

"What is that?" my brother said with a bit of disappointment (or disgust).

"Pam, I'm sure it tastes great," Bill said, seeing I was fighting back tears. He noticed my feelings were hurt by my always honest (and sometimes blunt) brother. "Let's pray."

Bill prayed such a spiritual prayer. He either knew this was a semi-sacred moment, or he was thinking the meal needed a miracle. If Jesus could change water into wine, would He change chicken in gelatin into a Pizza Hut pizza?

I dished them each up a big slice. Each wedge was kind of like a clear piece of gelatin pie. To my disappointment, it fell apart just like the green Christmas tree Jell-O. *That's okay,* I thought. *It will still taste fabulous.*

Bret took a bite. He swallowed really hard and gulped down about half a glass of milk. He looked straight at Bill with a look that said "I dare you to." Bill looked petrified. He looked at me and read the message on my face: *Please love me! Please love my cooking because I'm a new bride!* Bret was sending Bill a subliminal message: *Run while you still have a chance!* With the same gusto that one musters up to gargle with Listerine, Bill took a bite. He paused thoughtfully. I am sure he was weighing out his choices: *If I lie, will God punish me? Is it worth it to tell her the truth? How will the rest of the evening turn out?*

"Interesting," Bill sputtered out, reaching for his glass of milk. He took a sip. "What did you call this again?"

"Pheasant Under Glass. See, it's right here in this magazine." I held up the magazine. Pictured there was a perfectly formed, irresistible meal. It looked absolutely nothing like my tasteless concoction.

"What do you think, honey? What do you think, Bret?"

Silence! Neither of these normally courageous men was about to go first.

"Pam," Bret ventured out, "you know Mamma always taught us that if you can't say anything nice…well…"

"It can't be that bad! Let me try it!" I said defensively as I blinked back the tears.

I took a hopeful bite. The consistency was similar to the gooey stuff surrounding Vienna sausages or Spam. Other than a faint onion flavor, it was completely without taste. It is amazing how many thoughts can flash in your mind in an instant. Within a few seconds I remember thinking, *I should have known this wouldn't turn out. I have a hard time with macaroni and cheese—and I thought I could make this? Bill and Bret are just being nice. They should be telling me this is inedible. They probably want to rescue all of us from having to survive this meal. I should accept the fact that I'm not much of a cook and my efforts can be better used elsewhere. This stuff is horrid.*

As I fought back an automatic gag reflex, I blurted out, "Oh my gosh! This is horrible! I don't think I'd eat this if it was the last bit of food left on the planet and I was coming off a 40-day fast!"

Bill let out a huge sigh of relief and then laughed.

Bret said, "Oh, I'm so glad you said that, Pam. Because you and Bill are giving me a roof over my head, I wasn't going to say anything to hurt your feelings. I was just looking for a way to sneak this stuff out without eating it."

I started to laugh—then I started to cry. We had almost nothing else in the house to eat. I probably could have found some cereal or a can of chicken noodle soup. Payday was a long way off, and I had splurged on my fancy Pheasant Under Glass ingredients. "What are we going to do? You can't eat this, and I don't think we have much else around here."

My brother piped up, "You took me off the hook from having to say anything, so why don't I treat for Burger King?"

"Great idea! Thanks, Bret!"

As I dashed out of the dining room to brush my teeth and get the tasteless slime out of my mouth, I heard Bill whisper, "Thanks, man. I owe you one."

After the Burger King run, my single brother volunteered to drop us off and go play some basketball with his buddies at the park. He knew that Bill might have his hands full handling my emotions.

I learned that failed Pheasant Under Glass doesn't necessarily ruin the *amore*. From the first bite, Bill had loaded me with compliments and excuses to keep me off the hook. He complimented me for trying something new. He assured me everything was okay and reminded me of what he liked about me.

Bill lavished so much affection and affirmation on me that I reverted back to my mental picture of lounging on a chaise lounge by the pool, waiting for my prince to drive up in his Jag and whisk me to the bedroom. We had no Jag, and my prince smelled vaguely like the inside of an auto mechanic's toolbox, but we did have a bed and Hank Williams tunes on the radio. What more could a girl want? Who needs Pheasant Under Glass anyway? Not me! *Play on, Hank!*

Decide to Be Positive

Just as Bill could choose how he responded to "Chicken Under Gelatin," we each can choose the way we handle life circumstances, our mate's moods, and our own emotions. When life is challenging, when circumstances are difficult, when our mate or our children aren't acting well, we can each still choose to be positive. Here are some ways to regroup and recover from an emotional disaster:

1. Test the waters. Don't say a thing. Just give him a hug, squeeze his knee, or pat his hand. Sometimes the best things in life are unsaid. To remember this principle, consider this little poem:

To keep a marriage brimming
With love in the loving cup—
When you are wrong, admit it,
And when you are right, shut up!

2. Look for a positive. Anything positive—even, "Sure is nice weather today, huh?" In fact, one researcher discovered that the more positively couples rated their communication, the more satisfied they were with their relationship. Marriage conflict specialist John Gottman found that satisfied married couples average five positive interactions to every one negative interaction. Decide to have a positive attitude, and positive words will flow from it.

3. Try to encourage. Look for something that is good. Say some word of affirmation. Bill often says things like, "That's okay, Pam. I'd rather be here with you in this situation than with anyone else, anyplace else." When Bill blows it somehow, I usually say something like, "That's okay. You are a really great man, and this is such a small thing." Spontaneously list your spouse's best traits. (Who cares if you can't cook if your husband calls you "one red-hot mamma!")

4. Look for the humor. Avoid the cutting humor that can slice a heart, but look for the inside joke. Remember a worse situation and make reference to it. We travel quite a bit, and at times we eat some pretty unique foods and are placed in some really unique circumstances. To keep our attitudes up, one of us might say, "This is better than Pheasant Under Glass!" In our survey of couples who have long-term, happy marriages, nearly everyone mentioned the need for a good sense of humor! King Solomon, known as the wisest man in history, says, "A cheerful heart is good medicine" (Proverbs 17:22), and "Pleasant words are a honeycomb, sweet to the soul and healing to the bones" (Proverbs 16:24).

5. Keep it in perspective. When someone has cancer or we've just lost a loved one, we remember that everything else is just an obstacle to overcome. My friend Debbie, a career military wife, gives young, stressed wives great advice when hit with a tough circumstance: "Just adapt and overcome." We asked the long-term, happily married couples in our survey their advice to newlyweds, and a number of them used the same phrase: "Don't make mountains out of molehills." Before you raise the roof over some issue, ask yourself, *Will this matter ten years from now?* Usually it won't matter in a few hours from now! I often ask myself, *Is Bill's way immoral or illegal?* (Of course, the answer is always no, so as often as possible, I try to defer to him as a gift of love.)

6. *Go to plan B.* Offer alternative suggestions and solutions. If things are really tense, you might want to simply hold your spouse for a while and then ask, "Are you ready to brainstorm some alternatives yet?" When Bill and I were newlyweds, Viva towels had a commercial that tested their towels' toughness with others. In a tight spot, when we didn't know what to do next, one of us would ask, "What shall we do now?" The other might answer with a smile, "The Viva towel test?" Of course it wasn't the real answer to the real issue or problem at hand, but it usually lightened the mood and made us laugh so we had a better attitude. It gave us the opportunity to regroup, put our thoughts together, and come up with a new plan or solution to the real issue.

7. *Walk it off!* If your mate has a severe emotional meltdown, offer to take the kids to the park. (They probably want to escape too!) Vacating the premises sometimes gives God some space to quietly work on your spouse. God's healing and encouragement can be powerful. Draw her a bath, light some candles, turn on some soft music, and pray for her. Give him a safe place to escape and cool down. The garage, the tennis court, the golf course, or the basketball court might be a place where he can mentally regroup. Or find a way to relax together. Take a walk, go on a bike ride, or water the lawn. An interesting side note from our survey of long-term married couples is that many of them mentioned that buying a hot tub was one of the best investments they made for their marriage. One couple said, "We found out the silent treatment did not work, so we finally learned to communicate and share how we both felt. When we got our hot tub, we sat in it at night, shared how our days went, and talked about the things that bothered us before they became big issues."

8. *Hey, look over there!* Offer up a distraction: the movies, a shopping trip, or lunch out. For many women, a trip to Starbucks for a cappuccino, a stop at Crate and Barrel, some lotion from Victoria's Secret, or any kind of chocolate might do the trick. For a man who is upset or angry, a trip to the batting cages to let him get his aggressions out might help a bit. I saw a healthy pattern in my grandparents, who were married for more than 60 years. The more angry they were at each other, the harder they would work. When Grandma was really ticked, the house became spotless. When Grandpa thought Grandma was unreasonable, a new barn might just go up! One counselor once said to us at a conference, "If you have to choose dysfunctions, choose workaholism over depression. At least you'll have something to show for it after the emotions are gone!"

9. *Mia culpa.* If the emotional meltdown was your fault, apologize. I once helped the husband of one of my best friends throw a surprise fortieth birthday party for her. He was so stressed over trying to keep it a secret and hide all the details that he just wasn't acting himself. She became angry in response. In the middle of an argument the night before, she drove off in a huff. She was upset because she thought he wasn't going to do anything special for her birthday! Not wanting to spoil the surprise, he just took all the ranting, raving, and emotions. He finally offered to take her and the kids to a nice dinner and the movies. To pull off the surprise, he said they needed to stop by her friend's house on the way. Well, when my 40-year-old friend walked into her surprise party, she let out an excited gasp of joy. Then she immediately threw herself into her husband's arms and cried out an apology in front of her roomful of guests: "I am so sorry!" She knew a wise principle: The bigger the faux pas, the bigger the apology should be. Guys learned long ago that candy, flowers, and diamonds are good ways out of the doghouse. Remember, no husband has ever been shot while doing the dishes! So if you lost it emotionally on your spouse, try to think of a sincere, creative way to make amends. I once saw a huge white bedsheet with "I'm so sorry, Paula!" spray painted in big bold letters.

I don't know what the guy's mistake was, but it must have been pretty big. I hope Paula forgave him.

10. Keep short accounts. Passionate couples can ride the emotional roller coaster of life together. Couples who choose to let the past reside in the past get a fresh start with each other regularly. Couples who let resentments build up find that even the smallest infractions can create major conflicts. One husband offered this toast to his wife at an anniversary party: "Here's to a good sense of humor—and a short memory! May we never forget what is worth remembering or remember what is best forgotten."

11. Oh, dear Lord! Most importantly, pray! Our relationships with one another take place at all levels. They are physical, emotional, social, and spiritual. Sometimes we simply need to reconnect with the One who made us. You may offer a simple prayer, such as "Jesus, please give us a different way of looking at our situation." God might just send you a creative idea to save the day.

Same Phone, Same Address

Author Phil Callaway writes this of his twentieth wedding anniversary:

> Last August my wife, Ramona, and I celebrated 20 years of married life—most of them good ones…I suppose there are a hundred reasons we still share the same phone number and address. Here are my top five:
>
> *1. We left no alternatives.* The first three years of our marriage were miserable. Until I got a divorce—a divorce from loving myself and seeking my own way. What a difference it's made. Finding the right person, I've since discovered, is less important than being the right person.
>
> *2. We even golf together.* My wife enjoys golf about as much as I enjoy shopping for curtain fabric. Still she comes along

sometimes and cheers as I putt. Our fifth anniversary was celebrated on a golf course at her suggestion. Perhaps that's why I find it easier to move furniture when she asks. Or vacuum carpets. Or bathe the dog. One of these days I'll get up the nerve to enter a curtain fabric store.

3. We sweat the small stuff. Early on, I left mud on the carpet and whiskers in the sink. Worse, I often hurt her with a biting comment, or left my underwear where it landed. Small things can create quite a pile (trust me). So I'm learning to take care of the minor details, before they become major ones. If I'm last out of bed, I make it. If I'm late for supper, I call home. We go to bed at the same time even when I'm not tired and I kiss her lips before I shave each morning. Twice in the last year I lit candles in our bedroom, four times I've said "I was wrong," and just the other day (drumroll please), I even located the laundry hamper.

4. We travel together. Whenever possible, Ramona goes along with me as I travel across the country speaking. Sure it costs money, and I haven't had a window seat in years, but who cares? Our retirement savings plan may be smaller, but I'd like to grow old with someone with whom I share more than money, I share memories.

5. We pray together. One of Ramona's first wishes for our marriage was that we'd pray together. And I've honored this. To my knowledge prayer is the only reason the Bible gives married couples for abstaining from lovemaking. First Corinthians 7:5 says, "Do not deprive each other except by mutual consent and for a time, so that you may devote yourselves to prayer." Sometimes this has been a very short prayer! But bringing our desires, our dreams, and our concerns before God together has united us as a couple.

Lately we've been thanking God at night for His amazing grace. For taking two selfish kids who hardly knew how to spell *love* and drawing them close to Himself and closer to each other…For these 20 years, He gets the credit.

On our way to our overpriced hotel, we heard Huey Lewis and the News sing, "I'm happy to be stuck with you," and we both smiled and tapped our toes. But glue or chains don't hold a marriage together. A hundred tiny threads do. Threads like trust, commitment, kindness, humility, gentleness, respect, and flowers on an anniversary.

As we checked in, I told our hostess the significance of this day. Her eyes grew wide.

"Wow," she said, "that's a long time with one person!"

"Yes," I replied with a grin, "but it would have been a whole lot longer without her."[1]

Decide to Communicate
with Kindness

Love is kind.

*Married life is very frustrating. In the first year of mar-
riage, the man speaks and the woman listens. In the
second year, the woman speaks and the man listens. In
the third year, they both speak and the neighbors listen.*

Honey, I'll meet you at noon at Linda's. We'll drop off Brock, and
then we'll go together to the doctor appointment, ultrasound,
and hospital tour."

"Sounds great!" Bill chimed back from the family room.

The next day at noon, I was standing outside Linda's house with
two-year-old Brock on my hip. I rang the doorbell. She didn't answer,
but I could hear the phone ringing. I waited and waited, but no Linda
and no Bill. *Lord, I know I am pregnant and a bit forgetful, but I talked
to Linda and Bill last night, and I'm sure I said noon. What should I
do? I can't take a two-year-old to the doctor with me. He'd take over the
ultrasound machine! He already created some elaborate pulley system
with my drapery cord this morning and dumped out 3567 Legos to build
a "caswel, Mommy!" I have sung "The wheels on the bus go round and
round" for the last time! Lord, please send Bill and Linda!*

I desperately rang the doorbell again. I'm not sure what I was
hoping—maybe that somehow Linda would magically appear.

My watch read 12:15, and our appointment was at 12:30. I could
hear Linda's phone ringing over and over. "She needs to get home

and answer that thing," I muttered, desperately feeding Brock some Cheerios from a smiling Tupperware dispenser. *That smiling clown face isn't cheering me up. I'm almost out of Cheerios and time. Lord, You are God. You control the whole universe. Could you help out this pregnant mommy and just make Bill and Linda appear before me right now?* But, apparently, even this pregnant woman was not going to move the heavens.

I rummaged through my purse and diaper bag to see what entertainment I might have shoved in before I left home. The inventory included one matchbox car, a package of soda cracker crumbs, a box of raisins, and a *Goodnight Moon* book. *O Lord, can I manage one more round of "Goodnight stars, goodnight moon..."?* I reached in my purse again and found a squeaky basketball. *If I sit in the doctor's office with my fingers in my ears so I can't hear that incessant squeaking, that ball should keep him happy and drive the nurses crazy for 10 minutes.* I estimated all the rest of my stash would only buy me about 30 minutes.

Just thinking about the 84 ounces of water I drank for the ultrasound made me double over in pain and long for a restroom. I couldn't get into Linda's house to use her commode. I walked (hunched over, carefully keeping my knees together) and surveyed the perimeter of the house, checking for unlocked doors and windows. Even though I was desperate, I just couldn't picture myself hauling my nine-month pregnant body up and over those window frames.

The phone rang again. I began to think it was Linda trying to call me and tell me she was late. *No, Linda, I am the blond one who would think that plan might work.*

Just then Linda drove up. It was 12:25. She apologetically muttered some really good reason why she was late. I was so immensely grateful, I became instantly gracious. After all, she was watching Brock for free. All her children were in school, and she didn't have to volunteer to play ball and listen to that squeak! Linda transformed into an angel, Mother Teresa, and Florence Nightingale all rolled into one. I handed Brock off as I got in my car. The phone was ringing again, and Linda frantically unlocked the door and grabbed the phone. She immediately dropped the phone, ran out the door and down the street after me. She looked stressed and that made me panic. *Was Bill in a wreck? Was he lying bloody and bruised on the side of the road?* For a moment, I had sympathy for my very delayed husband. Then monstrous thoughts rolled through my brain, *Well, it would serve him right to be a bit banged and bruised up. It might have happened anyway if he showed up here right now.*

Linda was tapping at my window. "It's Bill. He's on the phone and worried sick about you. He said you were supposed to meet him at Linda's at noon." He had gone to Linda Brobst's, and I went to Linda Lamirand's.

The Choice Is Yours

Now I had a choice. I could create more drama and try to put all the blame on Bill for this mess. But we really didn't have time for the big fight that could ensue, and I concluded the best course of action was to accept some responsibility and apologize. With my bladder doing the thinking for me, I chose the expedient route. I waddled to the phone and in unison we said, "Honey, I'm sorry!"

"Bill, I am sorry, I really thought I said Linda Lamirand. Oh well, I'll just meet you at the hospital."

Bill replied, "Okay, angel, the hospital then."

I got in my car at 12:40 and had a 10-minute drive to the birth center. All the way there I replayed my original conversation with Bill. I was sure I said Linda Lamirand's. I whined and complained to God about the male species all the way to the hospital. *Guys just don't remember details, Lord. They must have husband's disease. They are always misplacing things, they're totally unaware of wrinkles in clothes, they put the milk carton back in the refrigerator with just a swallow left, and they leave their underwear and socks in the middle of the floor instead of the hamper.* I was on a roll. Never mind that my Bill rarely did any of these things—he was now in trouble just for being male.

I was angry at the entire male species, and my bladder felt as if it would explode. A *male* doctor had told me to take this ultrasound, a *male* technician told me to drink 84 ounces of water in an hour, and a *male* husband caused me to be so late. I justified my frustration by reminding myself that Bill had a big part in creating the pregnant state I was in. I was speeding and knew I deserved a ticket, but any male policeman who stopped me would have definitely put himself in harm's way.

I could imagine the evening news: *"We have a hostage situation on Union Avenue. A nine-month pregnant woman has taken a deputy hostage and has just released her demands..."*

I drove up to the hospital and thought, *What did I say? "Meet me at the hospital"? But Bill knows our appointment is at the birthing center. He was here last week at the appointment when we set this plan up. I'll go by the birthing center next door and see if his car is there. Nope. See, God? What would this man do without me? I'll go back to the hospital and see if he is there.*

As I drove in, I saw Bill at the front door of the hospital. I was steaming and ready to let him have it until I heard him say,

"Are you all right, honey? I know our appointment is at the birthing center. I already went over there and told them we are running a bit late, but so are they. But you said, the hospital, so I came over here to get you." How could I be mad at such a sweet and thoughtful man? *Lord, Bill is the best husband in the whole world! So what if he doesn't know the difference between a Linda Lamirand and a Linda Brobst?*

He lifted his arm to help me pry myself from the car. As I waddled over to the birthing center, I gripped his arm in pain. Wanting the rest of the day to go better, I asked, "After my appointment, do you want to get some lunch?"

"It depends on what time we finish. I have a premarital counseling appointment with a young couple."

"Oh, okay. We'll see then. What's the topic of this session with them?"

Bill sheepishly looked up and smiled, "Communication!"

Decide to Communicate with Kindness

Our miscommunication could have been complicated even more had Bill and I decided to be blaming, mean, belittling, accusatory, and angry. When we both made it to the doctor's office, we were frazzled, but we had no emotional baggage to sort through. We didn't have to waste valuable time adjusting our attitudes so we could enjoy learning more about this little life growing inside. No one had to play referee so we could get the task accomplished. Kindness protected our love.

A few key skills will help you communicate with kindness and protect your love.

Measure Twice, Cut Once

People in the construction industry commonly say, "Measure twice, cut once!" By rechecking the measurements, they avoid costly mistakes. In the same way, when we measure our words and recheck what has been communicated to us, we avoid costly relational mistakes. Most of the drama with my ultrasound appointment, including a good measure of the bladder pain from the delay, could have been avoided if I had made sure Bill and I had the same plan in mind.

"Bill, I'll meet you at Linda Lamirand's tomorrow at noon. Here are her address and phone number."

Then Bill could have repeated to make sure he got accurate information, "Sound's great—Linda Lamirand's at noon." Then he could have folded the address and placed it in his wallet. No drama, no trauma, just simple clear communication.

But in the heat of the crisis, we did do one thing correctly. We measured our words. When we got on the phone, neither of us tried to blame or shame the other. Instead, we measured out our comments and decided to stay positive and make the best of a bad situation.

Batter Up!

As couples learn to communicate, they usually experience a few strikeouts while up at bat. To raise your batting average and keep your hearts connected, try some of this advice from couples who have been there.

People who have long-term, happy marriages have found a way to make sure their spouse feels understood and supported. The learning process isn't natural, so it must be practiced. The couples in our survey who had premarital counseling and classes seemed to have an easier start. Other couples soon learned they lacked communication skills, so early in their marriage they went to conferences or read books and tried the suggested techniques. Some couples learned the hard way.

We asked couples, "How do you handle disagreements?" Here are a few of the responses:

Megan and Chuck, who have been married 22 years, were pretty honest in their answer:

- shout at each other
- separate
- cool off
- forgive
- talk things through and share our viewpoints
- let it go
- decide neither of us always has to win

Sandy and Paul, after 25 years together, have decided to compromise on their styles of conflict management. Sandy says, "We don't have too many serious disagreements. Generally, and probably to my husband's chagrin, we talk through it…and talk through it…and talk through it. His tendency is to just make it go away, and mine is to beat the issue to death, so we have to meet in the middle. But because of our shared faith in Christ, we are of one mind on most things."

Trish and Bill have decided in their 27 years together that the key is to "hear each other's opinions and listen to the reason why we hold our views." Carl and Brenda have been married more than 30 years, and they recommend a cooling-off period or "taking time for each of us to think the issue over." This allows emotions to calm before they hold their discussions. Karen and George, who recently celebrated their twenty-fifth anniversary, bring humor into this issue. Karen says, "We don't really have very many disagreements anymore. I'm always right. (Just kidding.) Actually, I usually say, 'Hey, I was just thinking about something, and I'm not sure which direction we should go with it. Think about it for a day or two and see what you can come up with.' That way, he usually thinks he came up with the idea, but it really was mine. Kind of sneaky, but it works."

We know this couple does not condone deception, but they let things ride while each person thinks through the issue. This seems to be a common denominator among couples who have been happily married for more than 20 years. They have decided they're together for the long haul, so every issue isn't a "make it or break it" matter. They aren't panicked to get a solution but are willing to take some time for prayer, contemplation, and mulling the issue over before coming back to the table and making a decision.

Clay and Jean married very young. We once commented to them how rarely people who marry at 18 and 19 are still married 30 years later. Clay said, "It isn't your age that matters but your commitment level." Clay and Jean have shown their maturity in the ways they have handled disagreements from the earliest years of their marriage:

- They discuss disagreements in detail unless time is a factor, and they only make decisions they both agree on.
- If time is an issue (and it rarely is), Jean defers to Clay.
- They pray for guidance and follow Scripture where applicable.
- They stay calm, and they both apologize quickly if they say anything unkind.

- They make sure the other person has said everything he or she wants to say on a subject.
- They try not to interrupt.

How Will You Decide?

The main point is that each couple decided how they will decide. Bill and I decided early in our marriage to delegate decisions according to who cared the most about the issue and who was most skilled at handling the responsibility. In the areas we delegate, the other person defers. For example, I make decisions about the boy's devotions, and Bill follows. What cars we drive: Bill's decision. He gets my basic input, but I am grateful I never have to go into a car dealership.

For major decisions and for highly charged emotional decisions (such as moves, career changes, choices about our children, and relational issues), we bring up the topic for discussion. We try not to do this when we are angry about the issue but only after we have prayed through it individually. We are not always successful at this, but we try to calm our emotions first. We talk, listen to each other, pray, and then repeat the process over and over until we get to an agreement. We decided to always try to talk sitting, looking at each other, and holding hands (at least one), and we begin and end in prayer. We have found we are less likely to throw things when we are holding hands! We are also less likely to say really unkind things when we are sitting close to each other and holding hands.

We don't want you to think all of our discussions are calm, peaceful, quiet affairs. We are two highly verbal communicators who are used to being on a stage or platform, so many of our discussions have started with a bit of drama. We both have strong personalities and communication gifts, and we came from two highly dramatic, dysfunctional homes. We decided early in our relationship that we needed to make a conflict covenant so that our propensity for drama would be held in check. Here are our rules of engagement:

1. Check the timing. Is this the best time to talk? If the issue is personal, emotional, or not for kids' ears, we wait and speak privately. If we are tired, we might begin the discussion but then reschedule for a time when we are better rested. Did one of us already have a bad day? We wait.

2. Check the closeness. If the issue is really important, we go away and spend time together reconnecting first. We talk after we rest, engage in some friendship activities, and enjoy times of intimacy.

3. Check the tone of voice, body language, and attitude. Am I communicating love in unspoken ways? This has been a huge learning process for me (Pam), as Bill is a very sensitive man. He is easily wounded by my tone of voice. I think I am being passionate or forthright; he interprets my demeanor as harsh and judgmental.

One day, after he said I had hurt him still again, I said, "Then teach me. Teach me how you want me to express myself in a way that I can release my feelings and give you the needed input but in a way that doesn't wound you. Bill, I love you. I don't want to wound you every time we have an issue we have to talk through. Teach me what I can do differently or what words I should use."

And he did. He replied, "When you say, 'You should...you need to...you ought to...' I feel disrespected." Then, if I raised my voice or used a certain inflection, he stopped me and said, "Pam, when you use that tone of voice, I shut down emotionally."

Allowing Bill to redesign how I communicate was difficult for me, but I believe it saved our marriage. I believe it paid big dividends later when I became a parent. My sons and I now enjoy great communication at a deep level because we all have learned healthy ways to express our emotions so others can listen and receive. I had to put my pride aside for the greater good and the greater goal of love.

4. Check in with God. When we make important decisions, we begin and end and sometimes stop in the middle to pray. If a conversation is going down a destructive path and we recognize we are hurting each other, we often stop and pray. Sometimes we also have to take a break for a few days. We use this time to check into God's Word, think about the situation, and process our own emotions.

The Best of the Best

We asked couples to list the best traits of their long-term marriages. Here are a few that were repeated among the surveys:

- We make room for each other.
- We maintain our own unique likes and activities.
- We aren't jealous.
- We stick together.
- We show respect.
- We trust.
- We have a good sense of humor.
- We love God together.
- We want to make our marriage work.
- We spend time together.
- We talk things through.
- We don't make major decisions without each other.
- We allow for our differences.
- We encourage each other.
- We both seek God daily, love Him, and seek His will first.
- We know that we will be faithful to each other until death.
- We share anything with each other as long as it is done in love.
- We consider the other's interests before our own (this is the fruit of the Holy Spirit).
- We believe that each has the other's best interests at heart.
- We communicate our love daily to each other.
- We do not concern ourselves with how much the

other person is giving or doing for our relationship. We look to ourselves to see if we are being the kind of people that God wants us to be and the other person needs us to be.

- We serve God together.
- We forgive.
- We are friends.
- We have confidence in each other.
- We enjoy all levels of intimacy.
- We are honest with each other.
- We practice hospitality together.
- We are best friends.
- We tell each other everything.
- We love being together.

Try a Little Kindness

We personally know many of the couples we interviewed (so we know they have happy relationships), and we are impressed by the way they talk to each other and about each other. We were struck by the repetition of the word *we* at the beginning of nearly every sentence. Every survey listed the friendship factor as key. The strongest marriages are made of two people who love being together. They are simply kind!

Being kind and saying kind things is a skill many couples have to learn. Some people were raised in homes that did not practice assertive, attentive kindness. Some well-meaning parents just get busy and forget to affirm. Stability alone is not enough. Some parents assume their children know they are loved, but the parents never verbalize their love or show physical affirmation. Still other parents are mean, hostile, and critical, so being unkind and uncaring seems normal for their children. Try using some of these affirming, encouraging terms to bring a bit more kindness to your home:

- It is so nice to have you around.
- I am a better person with you in my life.
- I can't imagine my life without you.
- Just being with you makes me smile.
- I love you.
- I value you.
- I appreciate you.
- I adore you.
- I think you are one of the most loving (or caring, or affirming) people I have ever known.
- We're a good team.
- There's not enough time in the day to love you.
- You are beautiful (or gorgeous, handsome, or strong).
- I feel beautiful (or handsome) when I am with you.
- I thank God for you.

One couple's advice to newlyweds sums this concept up: "Be nice! If something is not nice to say or do, don't do it. You should be the nicest person you can be for your spouse, not just for strangers or friends."

The Verizon Plan

Our use of cell phones provides an illustration of steps we can take on a daily basis to clear up other kinds of communication. If you are on a cell phone and you have a bad connection, you might do one of several things to get a clear line of communication.

1. Move locations. Have you ever walked around your home or office, trying to get a clear signal on your cell phone and saying, "Can you hear me now?" In the same way, to keep relational communication lines clear, change your position. Set your perspective aside and put yourself in your mate's shoes. Before you download your trials and traumas onto your spouse, check in to see how his or her day has been. You might wait until a better time to bring up a tough subject if his boss is unhappy with him, if she has interpersonal issues at work, or if he is working on an important project or case. A little empathy goes a long way. If you do have something important and pressing, offer to lighten your spouse's load with a kind gesture first: Bring him a cool glass of ice tea, run her a bath, or offer to take the kids out for ice cream to give him or her some time and space to regroup.

Don't say, "I have something I really need to talk to you about," and then leave. That might actually raise your spouse's stress level and make the whole situation worse! Instead, offer kindness and assess his or her stress level. If he or she seems relaxed, then say, "Honey, sometime tonight I have something I need to run by you. Can you let me know when you have a minute to talk with me?" You'll likely hear, "Sure, how about now?" or "How about right after dinner?" or "After the kids get to bed." At worst, you may get a "Can it wait until tomorrow?" If it can, wait. If it really can't, then explain. "It really is time sensitive, and I think it should only take us about ten or twenty minutes to talk about it. Is there something we can skip or something I can help you with so we can get just a few minutes together?" If none of these work, try these...

2. Call back. Sometimes when a cell line is full of static, you will hang up and call back. In the same way, if you try to communicate and your partner is misunderstanding or getting agitated or upset, simply offer understanding and then rephrase. You might say, "Angel, I can see this is making you upset. That was never my intent. Let me try to rephrase it." Then reword it. Make sure your conversations don't include these kinds of "static":

Accusations. Name calling, labeling, and swear words are all inflammatory to a conversation, so remove them.

Generalizations. The words *always* and *never* are sure to put your mate on the defense. Watch out for sentences like, "You always say that" or "You never listen." *Never* is a very long time, and using that word is a dramatic attempt to push buttons of guilt and shame in your spouse. The results will rarely be positive.

Rationalizations. These are excuses. They are often rebuttals or attempts to defend yourself and not take on any responsibility for the situation. This kind of tit-for-tat mentality will stalemate a conversation. Instead, offer a solution or system for working through the issue. "Honey, why don't you go first and explain to me how you are feeling and what you think is going on here? Then I'll explain my point of view, and we'll see where this leads us, okay?" In this way you are creating a new line of communication.

3. *Call the operator.* If your cell phone continued to have problems, you'd call the manufacturer or the operator to get help. If an argument is brewing, stop the conversation and call for help:

- Pray together for wisdom.

- Call a mentor. Find someone older and wiser who has been through this situation and can offer help or insights.

- Call a professional. A pastor or a Christian counselor can offer new tools or be a mediator in really tough-to-handle conversations.

The Secret of a Happy Marriage

A man and woman had been married for more than 60 years. They had shared everything, they had talked about everything, and they had kept no secrets from each other—except that the woman had a shoebox in the top of her closet that she had cautioned her husband never to open or ask her about.

For years, he had never thought about the box, but one day, the woman got very sick, and her doctor said she would not recover. As the man began to sort out their affairs, he remembered the shoebox and took it to his wife's bedside. She agreed that the time had come for him to know what was in the box. When he opened it, he found two crocheted doilies and a stack of money totaling $25,000.

He asked her about the contents. "When we were to be married," she said, "my grandmother told me the secret of a happy marriage was to never argue. She told me that if I ever got angry with you I should just keep quiet and crochet a doily."

The old man was so moved, he had to fight back tears. Only two precious doilies were in the box. She had only been angry with him two times in 60 years of living and loving. He almost burst with happiness.

"Honey," he said, "that explains the doilies, but what about all of this money? Where did it come from?"

"Oh," she said, "that's the money I made from selling the doilies."

4

Decide to Fight Fair

Love does not envy.

Marriages are made in heaven. But so
are thunder and lightning.

A husband and wife were involved in a petty argument, both of them unwilling to admit they might be in error.

"I'll admit I'm wrong," the wife told her husband in a conciliatory attempt, "if you'll admit I'm right."

He agreed and, like a gentleman, insisted she go first.

"I'm wrong," she said.

With a twinkle in his eye, he responded, "You're right!"

Admitting we are wrong and our spouse might be right can be incredibly difficult! A man and his wife got into a discussion about the homestead exemption allowed on their state tax. He thought he'd taken it, but she thought he hadn't. The man called the tax collector's office and told his story. A young woman said she would be glad to check, and she soon reported that he had not, in fact, taken the exemption.

"Would you like me to send the form to your office," she asked, "so your wife will never know she was right?"

Whether you're building a marriage or remodeling a home, conflicts are sure to arise. They are so commonplace that entire websites are devoted to one-liners about conflict in marriage:

- The most effective way to remember your wife's birthday is to forget it once.
- My wife said I never listen to her...at least I think that's what she said.
- I am in total control, but don't tell my wife.
- I married my wife for her looks—just not the ones she's been giving me lately.
- My husband bought me a mood ring the other day. When I'm in a good mood it turns green. When I'm in a bad mood, it leaves a red mark on his forehead.

Instead of dropping to the lowest common denominator, which will result in a downward spiral in marriage, decide to fight fair. Look for equitable ways to negotiate disagreements.

Why the Conflict?

How can couples go from bliss on their wedding day to complete chaos and conflict? Married couples experience times of discord and frustration with one another for at least three reasons.

The first reason is that you love each other! Your decision to act on your love and commit your life to one another has a startling impact on your life. Because you fell in love, your spouse has tremendous influence on your emotional well-being. Speaking for men, I (Bill) hate to admit that everything Pam says and does impacts me. It's just not fair! When she flirts with me, compliments me, and touches me in encouraging ways, my energy level goes up, my load in life gets lighter, and I am just plain friendlier. When, on the other hand, she is disappointed in me, criticizes me, or ignores me, I get self-conscious and inefficient. No one else has this same level of influence on my heart. She has the ability to make me feel instantly stronger or weaker. With a single phrase, she can inspire me to work harder or make me feel like quitting. She can dramatically raise or lower my confidence level with very little effort. This can be troublesome. I tell myself she shouldn't be able to manipulate me this easily, but I have found no way to resist. I tell myself to be stronger, but my resolve evaporates as soon as I see her. Around my guy friends, I have a clear view of boundaries and balance, but when I'm with Pam, the answer is always yes. I have often prayed that Pam will never truly understand the power she has over me!

When I (Pam) speak publicly, I get a real charge from the gracious response of the audience. The applause gives me confidence that I did what I set out to do. But if I walk in our home and disappoint my family, the joy of the event fades instantly. If some choice of mine has caused Bill or our family pain, my world gets rocked. No opinion on earth matters to me more than that of my precious husband, who has given of himself time and time again for my good and our family's best interests.

When this influence is positive and healthy, it is an awesome thing. Men have conquered evil kingdoms for the love of a woman. Women have sacrificed comfort and personal ambition for the love of a man. Couples have overcome overwhelming odds to build a life together because of the deep bond they share.

When this influence is positive, you can be quickly encouraged, energized, and motivated by your spouse. When this influence is negative, however, it breeds conflict. Everything your spouse does impacts your life, so the negative things can frustrate you, scare you, immobilize you, or discourage you. Your spouse can raise negative reactions in you like no one else. You may become more frustrated, more angry, and more disturbed with your spouse than with anyone else.

What I Love About You Irritates Me

A second reason you will experience conflict is that the thing you love most about your spouse is the thing that will irritate you the most. The person you married is both fascinating and flawed. Your spouse's good qualities captured your attention and drew you together before you were married. They are a big part of why you decided you could live with this person. But every good quality has a darker side that may drive you crazy. You will tend to see it as a flaw, but in reality, it is the same trait that stirs your heart and completes your life.

Let me (Bill) illustrate from our relationship. One of the traits I love most in Pam is her confidence. She has strong opinions, and I always know where she stands on issues because she consistently makes her convictions known. She's a fascinating woman to talk with because she's not afraid of new opportunities. She travels quite a bit and meets lots of new people. Because of this, she consistently has new stories to share with me and the boys. If she were afraid to venture out into these new arenas, my life would not be as interesting.

But this confidence has not always been enjoyable. Pam has a habit of making decisions for all of us in the family because she is so confident. She will assume we all want to do what she has planned. This is generally true because her heart is focused on doing good. But we sometimes wish she would at least ask us first.

I told Pam one day that I wanted to set up a desk at home so I could work more efficiently. We didn't have room for another office, so I was going to look for a solution that could be put out in the open. While I was gone on a trip with the boys, Pam bought a desk that folds into a piece of living room furniture. She even assembled it herself! I certainly appreciated her efforts, but it was not the style of desk I would have picked out for myself, and I had to redo the assembly. I couldn't say anything though because Pam had done this as an act of service for me.

One of the things I (Pam) appreciate most about Bill is his sense of organization. He keeps our finances in order and handles the routine chores of our household. He is easy to shop for because he likes the same things all the time. His sense of order drives me crazy sometimes, however. I travel more often than he does, so he will often clean the house while I am gone. I'm not talking about washing the windows and vacuuming the carpets—I'm talking about going through our stuff and throwing things away! I admit that I like to file in piles.

I know this frustrates Bill, but I can always find what I am looking for. I keep things I know I will use someday. Bill sees what he thinks is a useless collection of papers or magazines, and in the trash it goes—without asking me! I can't tell you how many times I have come home from a trip to missing resources. Why can't he just leave my things alone?

We would both like to get rid of the dark sides of what we love about each other, but we know they are inextricably connected to the bright sides. To wipe out the part we don't like would wipe out the trait completely. I (Bill) don't want Pam to give up her confidence, and I (Pam) don't want Bill to start living haphazardly. We only wish life could be simpler!

Your spouse undoubtedly inspires you and irritates you. You may have a very precise partner who keeps your financial records with clean efficiency but is so rigid you feel confined. Your spouse may be so socially adept that you feel she spends time with everyone except you. Every good trait has a frustrating side because we are all imperfect. As a result, I (Bill) often start conversations with Pam with the following statement, "Pam, something I love about you is irritating me, and I need to rediscover it. Will you help me?"

Your Humanity Is Showing

A third reason you will experience conflict is that you are human! You were born with a corrupted nature, and so was your spouse. As a result, you are prone to be selfish, proud, and controlling. Your relationship will deteriorate unless you put deliberate, humble, and focused energy into it. The Bible is very clear that we are all working from a deficit in our pursuit of good relationships:

> What shall we conclude then? Are we any better? Not at all!…There is no one righteous, not even one; there is no one who understands…There is no one who does good, not even one…Ruin and misery mark their ways, and the way of peace they do not know (Romans 3:9-17).

Everyone who has built a house has learned to overcome a variety of obstacles—problems with the ground, problems with the wood, problems with the workers, problems with the budget. At every step, the challenges must be defeated if the project is to be finished. I (Bill) learned this lesson when we built our home in San Marcos.

I thought I knew how to design a house, but I had no experience with the type of clay that our house sits on. This is the most remarkable dirt I have ever seen. When it gets wet, it swells. It fills every nook and cranny around it and turns into a glue-like substance that sticks to shoes, shovels, and sidewalks. I had to dig a trench in this dirt when it was wet, and I literally had to scrape the mud off the shovel with a putty knife to make any progress. When the dirt dries, it shrinks, causing cracks to form throughout the yard. It also gets as hard as concrete. It is almost impossible to break up and at best forms the equivalent of clay rocks. It is the weirdest stuff I have ever seen!

I had explicit directions from the engineer, showing me how to design the concrete slab so it would resist the expansion and contraction of the clay. I followed these instructions to the letter and have had no problem with the house itself. But I didn't have any instructions for pouring the concrete for my front porch. I never imagined that what happened could possibly happen. Over the course of four years, my porch moved toward the street. Every year the ground swells and shrinks. Amazingly, the porch moved away from the house so far that I could put my fist between the house and the porch. The posts were visibly leaning! To solve the problem, I had to break out the porch, drill holes into the foundation of the house, epoxy rebar into the concrete, and install a new porch. It was a lot harder to redo it than it would have been to do it right the first time! But I didn't do it right the first time because even though the ground itself was prone to trouble, I was too ignorant and proud to ask for help!

As difficult as it is to say, this is how most people approach their relationships. The relationship is prone to difficulties, but we are ignorant of what makes relationships work and too proud to seek out good help. The end result is conflict, arguments, and emotional pain. Clayton Tucker-Ladd, author of *Psychological Self-Help,* has some interesting things to say about this tendency for marriages to struggle. He points out that "David Olson of the University of Minnesota, who has studied over 15,000 married couples, recently said that 50% of married people will never be happy, unless they get unusually good therapy." He also points out that "only about 25% of couples have 'really good marriages.'"[1]

Even when we try to express love, our humanness and fallibility gets in the way. In *Romancing Your Husband,* Debra White Smith shares one of her moments that required grace:

> I never intended to harm anyone. Honest. I simply wanted to pamper myself a bit, so I squeezed a lavish amount of baby oil into my warm bath and lay back to enjoy the moment.
>
> After my "moment" was over, I drained the oversized, fiberglass tub, dried off, and started getting ready for bed. My dear, unsuspecting husband, who is built like a football player, hopped into the tub and closed the shower curtain. Then, the strangest thing began to happen. I say, "began to happen" because the event was something that should have happened in a split second but instead it kept going and going and going. The first thing I heard was a hard thud. Then a bum-bum-bounce-conk-crash. Next, some undefined body part, more than likely a hand, elbow, or foot slammed into the blue shower curtain. It puffed outward like a mushroom. More thudding. A flop. A few knocks. And another body part assaulted the shower curtain. A roll. A rumble. The sounds of shampoo bottles toppling into the tub. Then, silence. Poor Daniel never uttered a sound during the whole ordeal.
>
> Before the initial thud, I had been about to brush my teeth. Well, let's just say that little chore was postponed. I stood perched in front of the tub, not knowing whether to laugh,

cry, or run! I have strong tendencies toward hilarity. So, I seriously contemplated laughter.

I heard dear Daniel attempting to stand. At this point, he still had not spoken one word. Then, he dashed aside the shower curtain and glared at me. Daniel's eyes are pretty much a normal shade of green. However, they had taken on a strange, monster glow, much like a dragon's eyes in a nightmare. The only thing that distracted me from his glowing orbs was the round, shiny spot about the size of two silver dollars on his reddened cheek. Baby oil, of course.

As the irate stare continued, I forced myself to keep my face impassive. I strongly detected that laughter at this point could be fatal. Finally, Daniel yanked the shower curtain back into place. Still trying to repress the hilarity, I bit my lips until they ached.

My husband turned on the shower. The warm water must have washed away his fury, for soon I heard a chuckle, a chortle, and then outright laughter. Realizing the coast was clear, I allowed my own amusement to spew forth.

Only when his shower was over and we were both weakened with laughter did I learn the "inside story."

"I just couldn't stop falling," he said. "Everything I grabbed was slick. I would think I was going to stop then I'd slide up one side of the tub and back to the other." He paused to snicker. "It was like I was a seal or something."

Thankfully, a crack in the bathtub was the only lasting injury. (Do I even need to mention that I have refrained from adding baby oil to my bath to the very day?)

One of the things that has kept our marriage strong is our willingness to laugh at our shortcomings and mistakes and even the times we have accidentally hurt each other. My husband and I are total opposites. We could spend our whole marriage criticizing each other for our differences. Instead, we often laugh at ourselves and at each other. It keeps the marriage vibrant and alive. There are no hard feelings for our bobbles and idiosyncrasies—only fresh joy.[2]

This is the power of grace—that gift one person gives to the other because of love. Grace and a good sense of humor go a long way in keeping love aflame year after year.

Finish Well

We sometimes approach our marriages like a child who gets mad and takes his feelings out on his favorite toys. We claim to love each other. We intertwine our lives together. We commit our hearts to each other, and then we take out our frustrations on each other. This doesn't make sense, but it is the common experience of men and women.

How can marriage partners resolve conflicts?

The first step is to commit to one another that you will finish every argument. Most people think that an argument is over when they have solved the problem at hand. This is seldom true. The real goal of the argument is to reestablish an atmosphere of support in the relationship. You can solve some of the problems in your life, but others will never have a satisfactory solution. For example, we know friends who have special-needs children. These kids are a consistent strain on the marriage relationship, and they will never get better. For them, the problem is not going away anytime soon. If they need to "solve the problem," they will be forever frustrated. On the other hand, if the goal is to establish a supportive atmosphere, their arguments can continually work for them.

Choose Your Style

The second step is to choose your conflict style. Many people believe that a happy marriage is one where the home is peaceful, with little arguing or disagreeing. This sounds good at first, but it is not realistic. The truth is that couples discover stable relationships in various forms. Relationships fall into certain categories with regard to conflict resolution.

Negotiators

These are the couples who like to brainstorm. They look for new ways to solve problems. They like to explore options, ask other people for their opinions, and research books and magazines about their situation. Discovering different ways to approach a problem gives them a sense of security. When they have solutions to choose from, they feel confident they can choose the best option available. These people resolve problems methodically, and they often put discussions on hold until they can gather more information.

Bret and Erin are good examples of negotiators. "We look at a situation and categorize it. Is this a spiritual problem, a parenting problem, a personal preference, or a strong opinion? We defuse the potentially explosive timing element. We are committed to each other for life. Therefore, if the problem takes a day, a week, a month, or a year to fix, we can wait. We ask ourselves, 'Is this a hill to die on?' Some issues are, others are not. Only moral, scriptural issues are worth dying for—all else is just a disagreement. Sometimes we just choose to agree to disagree. I (Erin) don't care for Willie Nelson music, but I bought Bret one of his CDs anyway because he loves it.

"We have no guarantee of tomorrow. So if at all possible, compromise. Give up your right to be right all the time. Settle the issue and get to the making up! It is better to walk away more in love than to regret your anger if tomorrow doesn't come for the two of you.

"We have had two seasons of difficulty. One was after the kids started coming. Bret had to give up his dream of being a rancher to work at a steady job in the oil fields of Bakersfield, something he swore he would never do. I (Erin) handled it by first realizing that this was not as much of a career crisis as it was a spiritual crisis. I (Bret) felt that God had let me down and was asking too much of me (to give up my dream)."

Erin explains, "Bret did not like God very much during that time, and it flowed over into all the other relationships in his life—especially ours. I listened to wise counsel from my mom and sister-in-law, and I began praying for Bret instead of trying to be the Holy Spirit. I prayed God would speak to his heart with affirmation and love. I asked God to give Bret insight into the plans God had for him. I pleaded with God to confirm the desires of Bret's heart, even if he did have to leave them for a time. I also prayed that God would bless Bret with amazing success in his new job. I figured that would help his ego and make him feel less of a failure. Then I loved Bret—regardless of his mood. I tried to listen and give him room to grow spiritually by any means that would work best for him. I tried not to dictate what I thought he should do to get closer to God. God answered every single prayer.

"It took about five years, but God was faithful to us, and we are now able to talk about that time in our lives as an example to the Sunday school class that Bret teaches—and he is a wonderful teacher! The men see that Bret speaks from his heart and his experience. That makes them feel safe to look in their hearts and look at each of their own experiences and learn.

"The second difficult season was more recent. This time I (Erin) was the one who needed to learn a lesson. I entered the period that Pam and Bill talk about when a woman wants to save the world. I had done the baby, toddler, and house stuff. All the kids were in school most of the day. Housework only took a few hours a week, and I was wondering if this was all there was for me."

Bret says, "Erin began spending more and more time working at church and other ministry-related projects. This began slowly—accepting a bigger responsibility in the music department, helping a pastor with something, participating on the ministry board, teaching drama at church. Soon the responsibilities took not only her time during the day but up to four nights a week as well. She was soon on a roller coaster of 'good things' and neglecting our relationship. She admitted later that she was taking advantage of my unconditional love for her. I patiently tried to tell her that all of this was killing me. But she thought she was making a difference, influencing people's lives for eternity. She was fooled by the false conclusion that no one else was willing to do the jobs!"

Erin continues, "It was not until Bret awoke at three a.m. one morning with symptoms of a heart attack that I was able to stop the roller coaster I was on. On that day I realized that all the other stuff would just have to do without me because I could not do without Bret.

"This has been a huge growing time for me spiritually. I have learned that my first calling was and is to be Bret's helpmate in every area of his life. In doing so, I have experienced more joy, fulfillment, and contentment than I ever thought possible. Grace means that I am able to serve God when I feel His call, not whenever others need my help. God will be pleased with me, regardless. I am called to set an example to my girls of how to be in a loving, lasting, and faithful (with my time, attention, thoughts, and body) relationship with Bret. I want them to have that picture in their hearts when they enter marriage. These two 'calls' are all that I am told to do in the Scriptures. Everything else is accomplished according to the joint calling Bret and I share. If Bret doesn't agree, we don't do it. We are led by one Holy Spirit, who brings unity. If a ministry decision is not met with unity, then it is not for me. I want to stand before God and hear Him say that I faithfully helped the man God chose and designed for me. In doing so I have pleased Him and given others a full picture of what God intended marriage to be."

Debaters

These couples are loud and love to argue. From the outside, they look contentious and out of control. People are amazed that these couples even like each other. They may argue passionately, but they know how to make up passionately!

Peter and Carrie are this type of couple. They are both extroverted, task-oriented people. They are both natural-born leaders who like to be in charge. Rarely will two people with this personality marry one another because they both want to lead most of the time. They both have opinions about everything. They have a natural tendency to think that life is better for everyone when everyone agrees with them. Introverts tend to interpret their actions as proud and stubborn. In reality, they just want some control of the decisions that affect their lives. When they have no say in decisions, they feel out of control.

As a result, they are very willing to talk things through until they both get a say in what is going to happen. They can have arguments that few relationships can handle.

Peter and Carrie worked through one of these arguments one night. They were trying to figure out whose education they would finish first. They married in their midtwenties and were both only partially done with their college education. They only had enough money to work on one degree at a time, so an argument broke out. They were both concerned that one of them would never finish.

"I need to get my degree so I can provide for our family," Peter said first.

"I know that, but you aren't going to give birth to our children. If I don't get my degree before I get pregnant, I will never finish," Carrie aggressively replied.

"You could always go back to school when the kids are in school," Peter shot back, undeterred by Carrie's compelling tone of voice.

"You know my clock is ticking!" Carrie said.

"Your clock? What are we talking about?" Peter asked with obvious frustration in his voice.

"My biological clock! You know I can only have kids for so long."

"I know that, but your clock isn't going to run out tomorrow. Don't you think you are overreacting?"

"Overreacting? Do you want to see overreacting?"

With that, Carrie stormed out the door and got in her car. Peter followed her out, and they picked up the argument in the driveway. They partially resolved it in front of their house and then took it inside for about another hour. A lot of couples would be deeply hurt over an interaction like this. When Peter and Carrie were all done arguing, they embraced one another and enjoyed each other for the rest of the week. When they talk about that night now they just laugh!

Peacekeepers

These couples have figured out how to agree to disagree. They don't argue over much, but they also don't ignore issues. They easily defer to one another. These couples appear to everyone else to be naturally happy. Kim and Yvonne are just this kind of couple. Listen as they describe the simplicity of their life together:

"I (Yvonne) don't think we have had a really difficult season. We have had money problems, and that's always hard. Death of parents and major illnesses have been problems, but I think we always manage to remember that these things last for just a short time. Then things always get better. God is always in charge of these situations, and we just have to remember that."

Drama Team

These couples are very intense about life and forgiveness. They want everything on the table! They want to know the details and to talk through everything. They have aggressively accepted that life is imperfect, and they expect this from one another. They are consistently forgiving each other and repenting for their mistakes in a pursuit of excellence. Stephanie describes how this process has worked for her and her husband, Bruce:

"I think we are still working on this. I struggle to keep my emotions under control—I can get very vocal and worked up. We both still get defensive, so we have to keep at it until all of this immature junk passes. In the midst of this, however, we always hear each other out. I believe that when we both have been heard, we are willing to adapt to the other person. On most things, I get to the point where I go with Bruce's choice, as he is the leader and head of the family. If I know he has heard me and takes my opinion into consideration, I respect his decision.

"I think handling disappointments has been harder for us than handling disagreements. Trying to get pregnant for 12 years was very difficult on our marriage. We handled it very differently at first. I was more emotional and Bruce was more analytical. We frustrated each other. I wanted and needed him to be emotional, to cry with me, to scream with me.

"What helped both of us was to go to God's Word. It was our stabilizer. We looked at how God worked in various situations. We studied God's promises. We looked at the differences between God's actions under the Old Covenant and the New Covenant. It helped us both gain the greater perspective. We started asking more productive questions: 'What is God doing here? What are His purposes in this? How might He want to use us as a childless couple?' That focused our attention on Him and off of us!

"The most stressful time of our life, however, was when Bruce was counseling and visiting this lady who had tried to commit suicide twice. She was not a church member but had visited often with a friend (who asked Bruce to talk to her). I did not know who she was—I still don't. But when she started calling him at home in dire need of his immediate help, I got concerned. He got defensive. I got more concerned. I asked him, 'Do you find yourself thinking about her during the day?' He didn't answer—a dead giveaway.

"I reacted, calmly at first. I got up out of bed, went to the guest room, and closed and locked the door. He pounded and pounded. We had never spent the night in different rooms, and we tried not to let the sun go down on our anger.

"I finally opened the door. I felt hurt and betrayed. I knew he had not crossed a line with her, but just the fact that he thought about her made me crazy. We ended up spending most of the night sitting on the floor, talking about why we were attracted to each other in the first place, why we believed God had brought us together, and why we should stay together. It was pivotal for us. Nothing like that has ever happened since, and we are both very protective of him in the presence of other women. We have set boundaries for both of us—not being alone with the opposite sex, no frontal hugs, that sort of thing."

Survivors

These couples may not have great skills, but they always end up together. They may have past emotional baggage, or one of the partners may be overwhelmed by the demands of life. They probably approach their conflicts in different ways, and one of the spouses may work harder than the other at resolutions. They stay married by their sheer determination to stay married. They have frequent periods when they do not enjoy their relationship, but they keep finding ways to rediscover their love. Listen to David and Susan as they describe their survivor journey:

"We made decisions to get involved with a spiritual group wherever we were. We made decisions to do things together. We waited a few years before we had children so we could have time together. We each made moves to help the other develop our careers. Our best qualities are that we stick together, we show respect for each other, and we trust each other.

"I (Susan) try to talk disagreements out. David gives in and builds resentment. We have learned through counseling how to handle our disagreements more effectively. I have to be patient and wait for the appropriate time to discuss things, and David has to gear up to deal with disagreements. As we focus on building each other up on a more regular basis, disagreements are not as threatening as they used to be.

"A common faith is very important, but it has been difficult for us. If one relies on his or her faith for strength and the other doesn't have this to draw from, the relationship can feel lopsided and burdensome. On our own we run dry, but with God we can be renewed daily.

"Now is the most difficult season for us. The kids' activities gave us something in common. With the children now 17 and almost 20, we have to deal with us without them. We are finding we no longer have much in common. Disappointments in choices our kids have made are easy to take as failures unless we claim God's promises. This is a real test of faith and character. We have gone to counseling, and we just went to a marriage seminar. We've had to work hard to listen to what each other needs and make the decision to make this a priority. David is even agreeing to pray with me occasionally. I greatly appreciate this and give him space to do it quietly.

"Our children's adolescence was a difficult time that could have broken our marriage apart. We are not out of it yet. David slipped into depression and used medications to cover his pain, and I continued getting involved with activities and others' lives to hide my pain. The gap between us grew and grew. We have survived by finally getting help."

Servants

These couples identify who is most affected by the stress of their lives, and the other spouse commits to serve. During the struggle, expectations are low and sacrifices are high. The struggles are accepted as facts of life, and they are never held against one another.

Don and Lisa are good examples of people who resolve struggles through serving one another. They went through an especially difficult struggle after the birth of each of their two children. Lisa had lengthy bouts with anxiety and depression. After one of the births she even had some suicidal thoughts. Don accepted that his role was to be a supportive servant of Lisa during this time. He rallied their family and close friends to pray for her. His easygoing personality had a calming influence on Lisa as he rode out the storm.

This is typically how we function as a couple too. When we are in an argument, neither of us is very good at staying angry. We both make moves toward each other and toward serving or sacrificing to create a plan for connection. When there is any disagreement or tension, we know the other person is likely praying for the other and for themselves and asking God for a solution. We both apologize readily. Sometimes solutions to the issues take weeks or even months to discern, but we both continue to make every effort to move toward one another. One of us will often say, "I'd rather be stressed with you than living with any other person in the world." We often add hope by saying, "We'll get through this. God will show us how to love each other through it." We might have initial sparks and drama (especially from Pam, the self-proclaimed recovering drama queen), and Bill might initially withdraw or pull away in an effort to create some superficial peace. But neither of us can fire up or pull away for long. Our style is to take specific steps until we feel in love again. Then we can continue deliberating on the problem.

It Doesn't Really Matter

Research has clearly demonstrated that couples who follow any of these styles can effectively resolve conflict. Some of these styles will not appeal to you, but any of them can work. The key to their effectiveness is your ability as a couple to agree on the way you want to approach conflict. Discord comes when your expectations about how to resolve conflict do not line up. If your style of dealing with disagreements is effective for you...

- You will feel better about your relationship when you are done talking. You will have confidence that your future disagreements will enhance your relationship.
- You will enjoy the process of making up.

If your style of addressing problems is ineffective for you...

- You will feel worse about your relationship when you are done talking.
- You will start to avoid or dread serious conversations with your spouse.
- Your arguments will not lead to making up.
- You will become increasingly critical of one another.

If you start to see the negative characteristics develop in your relationship, you should seek help. A trained pastor, counselor, or ministry leader can be of great assistance in helping you discover your style of managing conflict. Do not wait for deep resentment or violence to develop. Start getting help as soon as you realize your current style is not working for you.

People Who Like to Argue

We spent quite a bit of time visiting with Pam's dad in our first two years of marriage. Pam and her father would consistently argue with one another. They disagreed vehemently on their political persuasions and were very vocal about their convictions.

Pam's dad would say, "The only people in Washington with any sense are the Democrats. The Republicans are making a mess out of things."

"They're not making the mess," chimed Pam. "They're cleaning up the mess the Democrats left behind. If the previous president hadn't made so many mistakes, we wouldn't be in so much trouble."

"The Republicans are out of touch with the common man," Dad would respond. "All they care about is their rich friends."

"It's their rich friends that provide jobs for the rest of us, Daddy. Open your eyes!" Pam would shoot back with a playful smile on her face.

This kind of bantering went on for hours. Once they were finished talking about politics they would shift to religion. When they exhausted that topic they would talk about how to parent children.

When Bill Clinton was elected president, we got a call from Dad. "Hey, kids, I just called to congratulate you. Someone from your generation is going to be president. I think this is just great. I think this may be the best thing that has happened to the country since I was a boy."

Pam was anything but pleased with the election results, and so she jumped in with her assessment of the state of the union. "Dad, you're being crazy. I don't trust him or his policies. I think we are all going to regret this day. I certainly didn't vote for him, but I guess you did. Daddy, I don't think you will ever learn."

"Charlie (that was Dad's nickname for Pam), one day you will mature and figure out just how right your old dad is."

After watching this interaction a few times, I asked Pam, "Why do you and your dad always argue?"

Her response floored me. "We aren't arguing."

"Yes, you are," I shot back. I was sure that they were hurting one another and causing damage in their relationship. I couldn't understand how a father and daughter could pick on each other like this and still like one another.

"No, we aren't," Pam demanded. "It may seem like arguing to you, but my dad and I talk with each other like this all the time. We love each other very much, and we never take these discussions personally. Actually, I find our discussions very stimulating."

I was amazed. I quietly realized that Pam would probably like for me to talk this way with her, but I knew I would never be comfortable with this style of communication. My parents and I could never have interacted this way. My personality is not drawn to this kind of contention, but it has never bothered Pam. Because of this, Pam has adapted her more confrontational style of interaction and asked that I teach her to effectively communicate with me when she feels passionately about an issue or we have a difference of opinion. I have also compromised by not taking everything Pam says so personally just because she expresses herself passionately. Together we have forged our own blend of conflict resolution.

Getting in Sync

Resolving conflict in an intimate relationship is like a team sport. All our sons have been competitive athletes. As we have watched them in action, we have noticed a lot of ways for teams to "get the job done." Each sport has various offensive and defensive schemes. All the schemes can be effective if everyone on the team is cooperative. The success of the coach is determined by his ability to get all his players on the same page in the execution of their game plan. The team's commitment to the plan is what makes the plan effective.

When everyone on the team is working in sync with each other, they are awesome to watch. Teams with less talent often defeat more highly talented teams because they execute with precision and cooperation. On the other hand, when a team is out of sync and its members are doing their own thing, they can perform far below their potential. The same is true in your marriage. If you are running different schemes, your efforts at getting past your conflicts are likely to be disastrous. If, however, the two of you are on the same page in your approach to conflict resolution, you will succeed.

A Conflict Game Plan for Handling Conflict

Just as the military has rules of engagement that outline how to negotiate conflict, we too need to have some guidelines in place. Consider creating a conflict covenant—a document that explains how you will handle disagreements. We have had one since we were newlyweds, and some days we think it has saved our marriage. These are some of the items in our covenant:

- Never say the word *divorce.*
- Never resort to hitting.
- Don't say words that you'd regret if your spouse was suddenly gone.
- Don't walk away until you reach an agreement.
- If your temper is out of control, ask for a time-out.
- Pray at the beginning and end of the argument, holding hands.
- Regularly read books about marriage.
- Attend a marriage event yearly.

We needed these rules because we both grew up in homes where rage ruled. We found if we held hands during our "intense fellowship," we were less likely to throw something! Some of our friends have a bowl of Snickers sitting on their coffee table. When they are in an argument, one of them asks, "Want a Snickers?" Eating a Snickers gives them time to cool down.

The last four items on our covenant are things that we will do if we aren't managing our conflict well:

- Call and make a reservation at a marriage conference.
- Call a mentor couple and set a time to meet with them.
- Call a trained counselor.
- Schedule a weekend or weeklong counseling intensive with specialists who help couples in crisis. (For a list of these resources see www.farrelcommunications.com.)

Finally, here are some verses you can memorize that will guide your communication:

Let your conversation be always full of grace, seasoned with salt, so that you may know how to answer everyone (Colossians 4:6).

Do not let any unwholesome talk come out of your mouths, but only what is helpful for building others up according to their needs, that it may benefit those who listen (Ephesians 4:29).

May the words of my mouth and the meditation of my heart be pleasing in your sight, O Lord, my Rock and my Redeemer (Psalm 19:14).

And remember, make sure you have plenty of Snickers!

From his side...
In the beginning, God created the earth and rested.

Then God created man and rested.

Then God created woman.

Since then, neither God nor man has rested.

From her side...

Love means never having to say you're sorry.

Except when it's your fault.

Or when it's his fault but he's too immature to admit it.

Or when it's the children's fault but he's holding you responsible.

Or when it's nobody's fault but he's looking for a scapegoat.

Or when...

5

Decide "We" Is
Greater than "Me"

Love does not boast; it is not proud.

There are two times when a man doesn't under-
stand a woman: before marriage and after marriage.
One advantage of marriage is that when you fall
out of love with him or he falls out of love with you,
it keeps you together until you fall in again.

—JUDITH VIORST

Some people say that the hardest thing for a couple to do together is hang wallpaper. We have not tried that, but we have had our moments with painting. With idealistic enthusiasm, we tackled every room of our first house—you know, the one that looked to us like a Ferrari when it was really a Volkswagen. We decided to use bright yellow oil-based paint for the trim in the kitchen. We had so much paint left after finishing the kitchen, we decided to paint the wood trim in the nursery with the same bright yellow.

The Saturday we set aside for the project started like any ordinary day. We ate breakfast together, planned out our day, and started in on the nursery. I (Bill) was painting the walls while Pam was working on the window. We pushed the nursery furniture into the center of the room and covered it with plastic leaving a space to walk all the way around the room. We didn't realize this also made a great hiding place for our 18-month-old son, Brock! We started painting during his nap that day. Since we were in his room, we laid him down on our bed, confident he would stay there until we were done with his room.

Neither of us associated the ringing of the phone with potential danger. We had not heard any noise out of our room, so we figured Brock was still asleep. I answered the phone call and discovered it was for Pam, so I went to get her. She went to the kitchen to answer the phone, and I decided to make lunch. Still we heard no noise from our sleeping child. Pam had a great phone conversation and returned to the nursery to finish her painting while I continued with lunch.

Pam walked in the nursery and navigated around the pile of infant treasures. Suddenly her shrill scream filled the house. Pam started yelling, "No! No! I can't believe you did this! Bill, come here! What do I do?"

As I came running down the hall I saw Pam carrying Brock with her arms fully extended. He was canary yellow! Brock had gotten out of bed while we were in the kitchen and opened the door to our bedroom. He had toddled into his bedroom and found the paint. He was so fascinated by it that he stuck both arms into the can up to his elbows. But then he didn't like the way it felt. Oil-based paint on his young skin must have felt like a million bugs crawling on his arms. He tried to wipe the paint off—onto his shirt and in his hair! By the time Pam got to him, his hair was yellow, his face was yellow, he was wearing yellow clothes, and he was crying yellow tears.

As they came racing down the hallway, Pam was screaming, Brock was screaming, and my mind was racing. First, my curiosity kicked into gear. How in the world did our son turn himself completely yellow so fast? I didn't know whether to be proud of him or mad at him! Then the handyman in me kicked into gear. We couldn't just give him a bath because he was covered with oil-based paint. I couldn't wash him in paint thinner because of his tender skin.

The answer was automotive hand cleaner. I remembered reading that paint was no match for good old-fashioned hand cleaner. Pam held Brock on the porch as I worked globs of the magic stuff into his hair. I slimed more globs on his skin, ignoring Brock's constant screams. I'm sure he had no idea what was happening to him—he probably thought we were going to make him permanently yellow! When enough hand cleaner had been slimed, wiped, rubbed, and smeared, we got the hose out to give him a good rinsing. On a hot summer day, Brock probably would have thought this was fun, but on this day he acted as if we were torturing him.

Of course, no self-respecting parents would stop with a hose rinsing after bathing their child in automotive hand cleaner. So, off to the bathtub Brock went in the arms of his mother. With warm water and soap, Pam cleaned every possible nook and cranny in that kid's body. She washed his hair three times. She found yellow in his ears twice. His face grew intimately acquainted with the washcloth. She finally decided he was presentable, dried him off, and got him dressed. The whole time he was either screaming, crying, or whimpering. He was so exhausted by the ordeal that he fell asleep once again in Pam's arms.

While Pam was taking care of Brock's hygiene needs, I went to the nursery to survey the damage. The puddle of yellow paint on the drop cloth had run onto the hardwood floor—the same floor I had repaired and polished so we didn't have to live with olive green shag carpet. I took about as long to get the room cleaned up as Pam took to get our son cleaned up.

And then it was time to talk. And we did what every red-blooded American couple would do at this point—we debated over whose fault it was!

"Bill, how could you let this happen?"

"How could *I* let it happen? What about *you?* I asked about Brock, and you said he was fine!"

"But I was on the phone. You should have been listening for him."

"I was listening for him, but obviously he is training to be a stealth operative for the government. You keep telling me about your woman's intuition and mommy instincts. How come they didn't kick into gear when we needed them?"

"Why do you have to be this way?"

"Because I'm scared!"

"You're what?"

"I'm scared! What if Brock had swallowed paint? What if he was really sick right now? What if we were on our way to the hospital? I hate the idea that I might ever lose him—or you."

"Yeah, I guess I'm scared too. I guess I just wanted to take it out on you because…well, because."

Selfless Indulgence

Fixing up a house can be traumatic, it can be rewarding…and it will test your relationship for all it's worth. In the same way, fixing up a relationship is hard work. It is a journey of selfless indulgence. To reap the greatest benefit from a relational remodel, you must indulge yourself completely in the pursuit without demanding that you receive anything in return. This, of course, is an unattainable goal, but by pursuing it, you direct yourself to the secret of great marriages.

The path to personal fulfillment in marriage is a commitment to the principle that *we* is greater than *me*. Think of it like a math equation: We > me. Deciding to keep the focus on *we* rather than *me* is no small task. A few building terms can help us direct our efforts.

Keep It on the Bubble

We built a two-story Cape Cod style of home. One day, while putting up the walls of the first story, we had to make sure they were *plumb,* which means the walls are perfectly vertical. In order for the second story to be added, the first-story walls had to be straight up and down, not just *look* like they were straight. One way to accomplish this is with a very long level. The top of the wall is moved until the bubble in the level is in the middle. The wall is level when you keep it on the bubble.

Another way to accomplish this is to drop a plumb line. That is how we set our walls. Bill was on a ladder and he lowered a plumb line from the top of the wall. A plumb line is a string with a triangular weight attached to one end. Bill lowered the weight until the point almost touched the floor. He moved the top of the wall until the point of the weight was in line with the bottom of the wall. My job was to check the weight and tell Bill whether the wall was *plumb.*

On one wall, I said, "It's close enough."

Bill said, "I didn't ask if it was close enough. I asked if it was plumb."

"It looks close enough to me. Does it really matter that much?" I shot back in defiance.

"Honey, I appreciate your desire to want to get this done. And I know these measurements seem tedious and boring, but every wall must be exactly straight. If we don't keep the walls on the bubble, everything will be affected. The floor joists may not fit. Cabinets won't fit right. And remember, the boys' rooms are upstairs. Do you want things right for the boys or just 'close enough'?"

"Oh, all right, I guess we need to make them right."

"So can you tell me, how many of the walls that we have just completed were exact and how many were 'close enough'? We'll need to recheck any you thought were 'close enough.'"

Thankfully, we were only on the third wall. With the other two I had been careful to be exact. Now I had a new reason to be thorough and do the boring, mundane work that would make our home a strong, lasting home.

Avoid Sky Hooks

Building relationships is similar to building a house. Relationships operate according to basic principles that must be practiced over and over again. Practicing communication, choosing a conflict resolution style, spending fun time together as a couple, creating a five-to-one ratio of positive expressions to negative expressions, and praying with each other daily are just a few of the basic skills that help marriages grow.

Instead of putting these basic skills to work, we have a tendency to make up our own plans and assume they are going to be effective. Bill was an architect major when we met, and he spent long hours designing houses. One thing he learned before changing majors from building houses to building homes and marriages was to avoid "sky hooks." Sky hooks are imaginary supports that don't work in real life. In marriage, when we make up our own rules instead of using God's, we are like building designers who rely on sky hooks to support parts of their building. On paper they work remarkably well, but they are really only an illusion. Careful planning is required to avoid these sky hooks because "There is a way that seems right to a man, but in the end it leads to death. Even in laughter the heart may ache, and joy may end in grief" (Proverbs 14:12-13). We can all too easily be fooled by the momentary peace in our relationships and not realize we are sowing seeds of disruption. Unfortunately, we meet couples all the time who are trying to live by relational sky hooks. Consider some of these sky hooks that people implement:

- Men will say, "I work hard to provide for my family. That should be enough." But history has proven that successful marriages require a balance of hard work and time together focused on each other.

- Women will say, "I don't think sex is all that important now that we have children and a full life." But healthy marriages are consistently sexually active.

- Couples decide to raise all their children the same way even though every child is a unique individual with a unique personality. Every child has a natural "bent" that is the key to motivating him or her.

- Couples will say, "We should live together first to see if we're truly compatible." But statistics say these couples are twice as likely to get divorced.

- Men and women withhold saying "I love you" because they think the other spouse already knows. But studies demonstrate a steady need for affirmation in intimate relationships.

- One of the partners makes consistent demands on the other, thinking this will bring order and direction to their marriage. But the best marriages run as partnerships where responsibility and authority are strategically divided up.

- Couples do things the way their parents did without evaluating the effectiveness of their behaviors. But mature relationships deliberately evaluate and choose their skills.

Bill has always persuaded me to avoid sky hooks in our relationship. From the very beginning of our dating days we were both desperate to build our relationship correctly. We both came from homes where the family patterns were ticking time bombs of dysfunction. If we didn't carefully unravel the patterns, we were likely to see some explosion in our marriage. We had to decide to keep the good and replace the unhealthy.

If You Fail to Plan, You Plan to Fail

When we dated, Bill had a notebook in which he wrote relationship questions. Every time we went on a date, we discussed that week's questions. I was determined not to repeat my parent's divorce, so I was impressed with this 20-year-old and his focus. From those talks, we created a framework for our relationship that was strong and sure.

When you build or remodel a home, you discover surprises. Some of them are good, and some of them are bad. When we built our home in San Diego County, we had quite a surprise just before we poured our concrete slab. After we dug the trenches for the footings, a large rainstorm came through our area. The trenches caved in, and all of the dirt that collapsed had to be dug out. The clay stuck to the shovels like glue, so as we mentioned earlier, we had to scrape the shovels with a putty knife. The extra work made our trenches a lot bigger than the plans called for, so we put a lot more concrete into our foundation than was necessary. We were sometimes frustrated, but we have no concerns about the foundation of our house. In the same way, we probably put more effort into our relationship than was necessary when we were dating, but we now have a strong foundation to build on in our marriage.

We have also experienced some interesting surprises in our marriage. I (Bill) grew up with a mom who was emotionally wounded sometime in her life. I'm still not sure what happened, but she needed to control situations, she suffered from paranoia, and her logic didn't always make sense. Pam grew up with an alcoholic father who was like two different people. When he was sober, he was as fine a man as I have ever met. He worked hard, was loyal to people, and encouraged his friends in their pursuits. When he was drinking, he was undependable, angry, and demanding. We both have an aversion to these traits and have worked hard to be aware of our reactions, but every once in a while they sneak out.

One evening, a group from the church I was pastoring gathered at the beach, and I baptized several people. We had finished the baptisms and were standing together about knee-deep in the ocean. Our three very athletic boys were in the water with boogie boards, enjoying the waves. Pam had to go home earlier than me because she had to catch a plane early the next morning for a speaking engagement.

She turned to me and said, "Bill, the boys need to get out of the water."

I looked perplexed and asked her, "Why?"

"Because I have to leave," Pam said, as if that was a perfectly good explanation.

"Well, I'm still going to be here," I said a little defensively.

"I know, but I'm not."

"Soooo…" I answered with a hint of sarcasm in my voice.

"So, the boys need to get out."

"No, they don't. I'm here to watch them."

"Yeah, but I know how you get. You're going to start talking with people, and you'll forget about the boys. While you're having a great discussion, one of the boys will be caught in a riptide and probably get carried out to Catalina."

At this point, I was freaking out. To me, Pam was not making sense at all, and I don't react well to women who do not make sense. I grew up with this kind of illogical thinking. I was encouraged to eat light-colored food because I have light-colored skin. I was encouraged not to work in an office on Navajo Street because I wasn't a Native American. I was told that people I didn't even know wanted to take over my life. When I moved out of my house, I vowed that my adult life would no longer be plagued by thinking that failed to connect the dots.

In frustration, I finally blurted out, "Let me get this straight, Pam. You trusted me to take the kids to Mexico. You trusted me to take the kids to Catalina. You trusted me to backpack with the kids in the mountains, but they can't swim in the ocean seven miles from home. Is that what you are telling me?"

Just then, the atmosphere between us changed. A knowing expression flashed on Pam's face. She responded, "Oh, my. I grew up not being able to trust my dad, and now I'm acting as if you're going to drop the ball just like he did. And you probably think I sound like your mom right now."

I agreed with her in my head, but I was not about to voice my concurrence! I may not always be the smartest guy around, but I do know it is never smart to compare your wife to your mother or to agree with her when she does!

Fortunately, we navigated that night well, but it was a good reminder to us that the shadow of our childhood will always be a part of our lives.

A Glimpse Behind the Wallboard

Our goal has always been to give our kids a bigger head start in life than we received from our families. Our parents passed some wonderful things on to us, but some of what we each grew up with didn't make a lot of sense. We are pretty sure that our kids will have much better experiences bringing their fiancées home to meet us than we had meeting each other's parents.

Bill first met my dad at a dinner when we had just gotten engaged. They didn't meet while we were dating because my father traveled extensively, and he never seemed to be in town on the weekends. Bill and I were living in different towns and only saw each other every other weekend. After he proposed, Bill moved to my hometown of Bakersfield, where I was attending college.

My father was a very loving, generous man, but he grew up in a severely dysfunctional family. Alcoholism runs through my family tree like sap. My father dealt with his personal pain by drowning it in a bottle.

Bill's first dinner with my dad went okay because my dad, dressed in his suit, came straight from work, and he was relatively sober. He loved Bill and wanted to give us some money for the upcoming wedding. He named an amount, and we thanked him for his generosity. Then he added, "Kids, why don't you come to my house in Stockton next weekend so I can write you a check? That way I can get to know Bill better and spend some time with you all."

The next weekend, we drove about four hours from Bakersfield to Stockton. When we arrived at Dad's, he wasn't there. He eventually arrived home from water-skiing with his buddies—and drinking. He continued drinking while he tried to barbecue our dinner. Unable to remain focused, he turned our dinner into a burnt offering.

He became upset, so I calmed him down by saying, "It's okay, Daddy. I didn't come to eat your food. I came to spend time with you. It doesn't matter to me what we eat. What if I just order some pizza?"

While we waited for the pizza, Dad drank some more. I thought, *Okay, regroup. Maybe we can salvage something out of our evening.* When the pizza arrived, I served Bill and Dad and filled their glasses with milk. The first bite went well, and I thought we were going to have a peaceful dinner. When Dad took his first drink of milk, however, he promptly threw up all over the pizza and all over me. I threw myself in front of Bill, trying to save him from even having to see this scene!

I (Bill) remember thinking, *Wow, Pam is in the club also. I have seen some pretty crazy stuff at my house growing up, and apparently she has also. I think I should probably be more upset about this, but sadly, it seems kind of normal to me. I better pray for Pam because she looks pretty upset.*

I (Pam) cleaned up Dad and put him to bed. Bill and I cleaned up the kitchen, and then we went to the park. I said to him, "We need to pray! My dad has a pattern. The day after something like this happens, he tries to buy me off with money. I want to honor my daddy for being my daddy because God gave him to me, but I also don't want these guilt strings and patterns to follow us into our new relationship. We're going to need some wisdom for tomorrow."

We sat in a park a few blocks down the street from my dad's house and prayed. After praying, we felt impressed to only accept the amount my dad had initially offered. We also decided we would expect absolutely nothing, just in case he was out of sorts. The next day, Dad had an alcoholic blackout. He didn't remember the details of what happened, but he knew it was something very bad. He wrote out a huge check. I could have had Princess Diana's wedding!

I handed the check back to my dad, and said, "Daddy, I love you. I will not manipulate you with your pain. If you want to give us the initial amount you said last week at dinner when you were sober, that is more than generous. Dad, we do not expect anything, but I do hope you will walk me down the aisle."

Dad wrote out a check for the initial amount and promised to be there to walk me down the aisle—sober. My daddy told me years later that was the first time in his life he felt unconditionally loved just for who he was and not for what he could do. I believe it was a significant moment in his spiritual journey that led to his own decision for Christ shortly before he transitioned from this life to eternity.

Under Control

Pam met my parents shortly after our engagement. I told Pam my mom talks a lot, which is true. She needs to talk a lot because it gives her control of conversations. When things in life get out of my mom's control, she gets nervous and scared. But I failed to tell Pam what my mom talks about.

My father is a generous, kind man who is a very successful aeronautical engineer. He is wonderfully easygoing and respectful. My parents met while they were students at the University of California at Berkeley. My dad then became an Air Force pilot. They traveled to France, gave birth to my sister in Germany, and finally settled in Sacramento, where my brother and I were born.

I never knew much about my extended family. Both my parents distanced themselves from their families before I was born. Almost all holidays and vacations were spent with just our immediate family. Spending time with relatives was a foreign concept to me—but Pam's family is big on extended family.

I (Pam) thought this was unique because I knew my cousins on every side. At our wedding reception in Idaho, Bill met almost 100 relatives in one day!

On the day I met Bill's folks, we'd only been at his home a few minutes when I knew something was different. The walls were all painted different colors. One of Bill's parents mentioned they were redecorating. His dad said, "Bill, you want to go to the hardware store?" So off the men went, leaving me alone with Bill's mom for two hours!

In that time, his mom talked about the reason all the walls were different colors. "We're looking for the color that shows up bugs the best." (It's baby blue if you really want to know.) Then she began to ramble around a variety of subjects. "I don't cook anymore because of the bugs. I put Clorox in the flower beds to see if we could kill them all…You know, I think someone followed me home yesterday…I don't think the Vietnam War really happened. I think the government just made it up and made a bunch of movies. I love Hollywood, don't you?…You know, I don't eat chocolate ice cream because I have white skin…I don't think we should eat at Bob's Big Boy tonight because you're not a big boy, I'm not a big boy, and you don't have any big boys!" I thought for sure I heard the theme music from *The Twilight Zone* playing in the background as the time passed.

My heart broke for Bill, his dad, and his mother that day. Obviously some significant pain was lodged behind the scenes, and it wasn't until nearly 20 years later at a family funeral that we found out just how much trauma these two talented and giving people had experienced in their own families of origin.

We both realized if we could survive the first meeting of the parents, we could survive almost anything in marriage!

On the brighter side, Bill met my mom by phone during our dating days. He called and asked permission to date me, which my mom still can't get over. He called again before asking me to marry him. My mother was a Christian, and she had done some significant work in counseling to recover from living with the abuse and violence of my father. It was awesome to have one normal encounter with in-laws!

Throughout our marriage, we have asked two very deliberate questions: First, what did our parents do that we want to continue doing in our generation and pass on to future generations? And second, what are the things we do not want to repeat in our lives, and what are we going to replace them with? We have come up with several items:

Family Values We Want to Keep

- Find a career you'd love even if you didn't get paid for it.
- Work hard.
- Stand up for what is right just because it is right.
- Be creative.
- Be a good citizen.
- Be involved in your community.
- Be loyal and generous to friends and family.

New Family Values We Want to Introduce

- Make God a central part of life rather than living independent of Him.
- Pursue goals and good friendships rather than alcohol.
- Rather than avoiding difficult people, help them to grow.

- Live according to goals rather than fears and pain.
- Help kids discover their unique gifts and interests.
- Commit to a lifetime of deliberate personal growth.

"We" Is Greater than Our Mistakes

The most important skill in maintaining unity as a couple is forgiveness. You will undoubtedly make mistakes, disappoint one another, and make some poor decisions. No one can deny that these things happen. The only way to keep the relationship growing in the midst of our humanity is to forgive. The apostle Paul gave us a staggering challenge: "Bear with each other and forgive whatever grievances you may have against one another. Forgive as the Lord forgave you" (Colossians 3:13). We designed six statements to help people work through the process of forgiveness.

1. I forgive (name of person) for (offense that was committed).

2. I admit that what was done was wrong.

3. I do not expect (name of person) to make up for what he or she has done.

4. I will not define (name of person) by what he or she has done. Instead, I will define him or her as someone who needs just as much grace in life as I do.

5. I will not manipulate (name of person) with what he or she has done.

6. I will not allow what has happened to stop my personal growth.

Andy Stanley explains that when we forgive, we list all the things the offending party has done and then stamp it with "Debt Paid in Full." We write on the list of grievances, "You don't owe me." It is very hard but very freeing to say to God, "They don't owe me an explanation. They don't owe me an apology. They don't owe me any restoration." Forgiveness frees you to go forward in life and forward in all your relationships.

Forgiveness is a vertical, private act between you and God. Reconciliation is a horizontal act between people who have been separated by a hurt or grievance. Reconciliation works best when both people have already walked through the six statements of forgiveness listed above. A relationship is more likely to be restored if the offending party says, "I'm sorry. Please forgive me. What can I do to make things right again?"

Often "what will make things right again" is an explanation, an apology, and a restitution of some kind that is freely offered. The key in this tangled and emotionally charged process of forgiveness and restoration is that each person forgives the other completely, not because anyone asks but because Christ forgave us. Forgiveness protects your integrity and your heart.

Each person should freely own his or her issues. This is not the time to rationalize, blame others, or duck your guilt. Truly repentant people will say, "I'm sorry. What I did was wrong. Here's why it was wrong. Please forgive me. What can I do to help set things right again?" Then they close their mouth and listen intently and from the heart.

Forgiveness is all about grace. Loving unconditionally. Love is wanting the best for the other person, regardless of the cost to you. Forgiveness costs emotionally, but bitterness and resentment extract even more from your life. Forgiveness is expensive—it cost Christ His life to die for the world's imperfection. But the payoff is priceless; no amount of money can ever repay that kind of gift of love. When you grasp how much God loves you, extending grace and unconditional love to others becomes a little easier.

Pam and I have had numerous opportunities to practice these six statements. Two particular instances involved money, a very common topic of concern for married couples.

Pam's Magic Beans

I (Pam) am a pushover for a slick salesman. I know that if

something sounds too good to be true, it probably is, but the idealistic instinct in me is not hard to trigger. When I was first starting my writing career, I was also finishing my degree. We needed some extra income to wrap up the school bill. I received an invitation to a free seminar presenting an idea for a home business, so I went. The promises the salesman made were amazing. He listed many people who had made money relatively quickly and easily with this turnkey business idea. It sounded so good, so easy. Just like Jack and the Beanstalk, I traded my cow for five magic beans. I was sure my beanstalk would reach the golden goose in the sky. But unlike Jack, I really did just get five boring beans, and no big business grew.

We have made a rule that we don't spend more than a certain amount of money without checking with each other first. But the salesman said we had to act immediately. I have always believed that God is never in a hurry, and big decisions are best prayed over, at least overnight. I believe in my heart I should pray with Bill over big decisions. But I went against my own conscience, and the Holy Spirit screaming inside, and even the advice of my friend who had gone with me. The salesman's enthusiasm and persuasion were too much for me. I jumped at the sales offer in the back of the room.

As I was driving home I was feeling bad, not so much for the desire to try an adventure but because of the way I did it. Instead of talking with Bill, I prayed a cursory *God bless me!* and not a prayer for wisdom or guidance. I walked into the house and said to Bill, "Honey, I'm going to tell you something, and I need you to respond with, 'I love you, Pam, and we will work through this.'"

As I shared my Jack and the Beanstalk story, I could read the disappointment on Bill's face. I know his heart was lagging behind his actions, but he dutifully gave me a hug and gathered me on to his lap. He bravely said to me, "Pam, I love you, and we will work through this."

Because of Pam's opening line, I (Bill) immediately thought the worst. Is it cancer? An affair? Is one of the kids hurt? So when she told me about the money, it didn't seem quite so bad. We didn't have the money to spend, especially on magic beans, but the problem was smaller than the other scenarios that had raced through my head. Her actions were unjustified, and I still needed to forgive her, but a little perspective makes forgiveness a lot easier.

I Need to Take a Risk!

I (Bill) have several friends who are big entrepreneurs. One came to me with an idea that sounded amazing. It was an investment opportunity with a terrific payoff. It sounded too good to be true, but I knew the guy. I knew his credentials. I knew his bio and his background. He had even spent some time in full-time ministry. He said he needed just a few more investors to make the plan work, and it would pay off in just a few weeks. He did say it was a risk, but it sounded like a calculated, well thought-out one.

I talked with Pam. We prayed. We weighed the options. I could tell she was hesitant because the money we would use was coming through her income source. It seemed to her like a whole lot of eggs to put in one basket. In the end she said, "Okay, honey. I believe in you, and I trust you. If you think this is best for us and our family, then do it."

So I went for it. Weeks passed with no payoff. Months came and went with no benefit from the investment. Years have now elapsed since I took that risk, and we will obviously never receive any profit from it. I tried to float Pam's hard-earned money upon the water, and it sank. I knew I had failed her. I couldn't explain my actions except to say I had stars in my eyes. All I could do was say, "I'm sorry," and throw myself on her mercy.

I (Pam) knew I had a choice. I could be resentful and angry. Bill had been wrong to spend money I earned in this way. I had plenty of reasons to harbor resentment. But I also realized that resentment would cause a rift. I would have lost not only the money but also something in our relationship. I had to ask myself, *How many times do I want to lose?* I had given Bill the green light to decide for our family. I didn't think I should now take back my blessing and cooperation just because the plan failed. I placed my pain and disappointment at the foot of the cross.

As I did, all the wonderful, encouraging things Bill had said and done over the years came flooding back into my mind. I told God, *Lord, this is a lot of money, but it's a small price to pay to be married to a man as wonderful as Bill.*

I remembered a story Reverend E.V. Hill shared about his wife when she was placed in a similar situation. She calculated that since E.V. didn't drink, smoke, or gamble as many men do, she was still financially ahead when one of his investments lost the family some money. I also thought of my own mother and father. My mom once calculated how much money my dad drank away. She figured it was enough to send all three of us kids to an Ivy League college! I decided Bill's bad investment was a small price to pay for the privilege of being married to such an honest and affirming man. I relayed my decision to Bill, much to his relief. We have spent a lot of time laughing about both of these financial sky hooks since we found the grace to forgive each other rather than carry grudges.

A young man excitedly told his mother he'd fallen in love and was going to get married. He said, "Just for fun, Ma, I'm going to bring over three women, and you try to guess which one I'm going to marry."

The mother agreed.

The next day, he brought three beautiful women into the house and sat them down on the couch. They chatted for a while, and then he said, "Okay, Ma, guess which one I'm going to marry."

She immediately replied, "The one in the middle."

"That's amazing, Ma! You're right! How did you know?"

"I don't like her."

Decide to Keep
the Sex Sizzling

Love is not rude; it is not self-seeking.

Kissing, *n. [1] a method of getting two people so close together*
that they can't possibly see anything wrong with each other

Every house needs to be decorated. It needs to be painted, carpeted, wallpapered, and furnished. In our hearts is a desire to put our own touch on the place we call home. Without decorations, the home would feel sterile and industrial. It might be sturdy, functional, and safe, but it would not be home.

In the same way, every intimate relationship needs to be decorated. Married couples need to have a sturdy, stable relationship to endure the challenges of life. But you didn't get married just to endure. You got married because you were in love and believed you could have a great time together. You want to be valued, loved, and treasured by each other. This is why God created sex and romance. Sexual intimacy is the decoration that makes your relationship uniquely yours. It is a secret you share with each other, a dance you perfect together, and an adventure you explore.

How do you develop a sex life that will decorate your relationship? What makes a great lover? What quality is the most sensual? What is the biggest turn-on ever? Is it six-pack abs? A curvaceous figure? Is it the way she walks? The way he talks? Is it his money? Her bedroom eyes? His power? Her fragrance? None of these things are as important as the decision to keep the flames of passion burning, the daily decision to make your intimate life a priority.

We chose to take the plunge because we were fascinated with each other. I (Bill) met Pam when we were in college. We were attending a leadership training conference with Campus Crusade for Christ. I first noticed Pam on the diving board in the pool. She was a competitive diver during her freshman year and had a distinctive style on the board. I remember thinking to myself, *God did a good job when he made her!*

I (Pam) remember seeing Bill at the pool also. He had long, curly hair. He came up out of the water and shook the water out of his hair. He looked just like the man on the back of a teen magazine I had seen. (I had shown my sister and friends the ad and said "I want to marry a man who looks like that!") I was captivated even though I didn't know at the time this was God's choice for me.

Part of the fun of intimate relationships is this ongoing fascination with one another. But sometimes the pressures of life can dim this fascination. You can give one another three gifts that will keep your interest growing if you give them consistently: the gift of *admiration,* the gift of *anticipation,* and the gift of *adventure.*

An entire book of the Bible is devoted to these three gifts that make intimate, sensual relationships a great journey together. The book, Song of Songs (or Song of Solomon), tells the story of a real couple. The story is so moving that God decided to include it in the text of Scripture. The book is so sensual that Jewish children were not allowed to read it until they became adults! Most people don't even know that a book this explicit is in the pews at church!

The Gift of Admiration

Men and women alike long to be loved. We long for the look of admiration in the eyes of the one we love. Our entire outlook on life is brightened by sincere compliments. We so long to be admired by each other that we often go fishing for compliments just to see if we are still adored. In the Song of Songs, chapter 2, we encounter Solomon and his Shulammite bride in a reunion after he has been on a business trip.

The bride begins by saying, "I am a rose of Sharon, a lily of the valleys." In Israel, lily of the valley is as common a flower as you could find. It grows everywhere—even along the roadside and in fields. She is looking at all the beautiful women around her and she has convinced herself that they are all fantastic roses while she is a dull dandelion. She is fishing for compliments! She wants to feel beautiful and knows that just one word from Solomon is all it will take. But she is too vulnerable to say, "Solomon, will you tell me I am beautiful? I am feeling kind of insecure right now, and your words always do the magic on my heart." Instead she says, "I am sorry you have to be married to such an ordinary woman."

But Solomon is smooth in his answer. "Like a lily among thorns is my darling among the maidens." Did you catch that? He's saying, "Baby, all the other women are like thorns compared to you! You are the only rose!"

She is instantly transformed from being self-conscious to focusing on Solomon! His words have made him wise, kind, and trustworthy in her heart. As a result, she responds in kind.

> Like an apple tree among the trees of the forest is my lover among the young men. I delight to sit in his shade, and his fruit is sweet to my taste. He has taken me to the banquet hall, and his banner over me is love. Strengthen me with raisins, refresh me with apples, for I am faint with love. His left arm is under my head, and his right arm embraces me (2:3-6).

An apple tree in the forest? How many apple trees grow wild in the forest? Not very many! She is saying, "My king, you are one in a million!" A marvelous transition has happened in their interaction together. This points to something that has been consistently demonstrated: Trust is the trait in a relationship that enables women to reach sexual fulfillment. A wife who trusts her husband with her heart will long for him with her body. Solomon's words have traveled from her ears to her heart.

She looks around her and realizes how very fortunate she is. She recalls that he has taken her into his banquet hall, and his banner over her is love. Most likely at this point, she is in the chamber that the king had designed and made especially for her. She may have climbed on to the bed in the middle of the room he built for her. I (Pam) picture her falling back, arms wide open, inviting her husband to join her as she looks up and realizes his attention to all the details that would make her feel at home. He may have acquired timbers from her homeland and plants from her parents' ranch. Her eyes are finally off herself and back onto the man who deserves her full attention. When she says, "His banner over me is love," she could be alluding to the fact that the best part of this new home is her husband being there.

She continues to use word pictures that communicate her desire for sexual intimacy. She talks about apples and raisins and how she is famished, "faint from love." She's dropping hints that she is starving for sex in the same way she longs for her favorite food.

Then she gives the compliment every husband longs to hear. She tells him he is a great lover! "His left arm is under my head, and his right arm embraces me." She might as well be saying, "Honey, I love it when you..." His left arm is under her, caressing her head while his right arm is embracing her, moving to the places that cause her pleasure and arousal.

Men love to hear they are good lovers, but lovemaking does not come instinctively. As the relationship grows, sexual interaction becomes more relational and less athletic. That's why couples who discuss their sexual relationship on a consistent basis achieve more satisfaction in their intimate interaction. This is also why couples who pray together on a daily basis rate their sexual satisfaction very high. The more relational the couple becomes, the more intimate their sexual expression becomes. Knowing this, we take time every year as part of our anniversary celebration to discuss our sex life. We ask questions such as these:

- What do you like about our sex life?
- What was the most interesting part of our sexual interaction during the last year?
- What did we do together that you hope we do again?
- What did we do together that you would prefer to not do again?
- Is there anything you would like to try (or try again) this year that would make you feel loved?

I Love You Head to Toe

Solomon has caught on that words are very powerful aphrodisiacs. As a result, he very explicitly lists the alluring physical qualities of his bride from head to toe.

> How beautiful you are, my darling! Oh, how beautiful! Your eyes behind your veil are doves. Your hair is like a flock of goats descending from Mount Gilead (4:1).

This is his way of saying her hair was streaming beautifully down her body, and her beautiful, pure eyes were peeping from under her cascade of hair. The goats referred to here were those with lovely glistening silky black hair.[1]

> Your teeth are like a flock of sheep just shorn, coming up from the washing. Each has its twin; not one of them is alone. Your lips are like a scarlet ribbon; your mouth is lovely (4:2-3).

The reference to her teeth meant they were white and none were missing. This makes sense because the next place Solomon looks is at her lovely mouth, which is compared to a scarlet thread. It is likely that Solomon is kissing and caressing as he continues his journey of admiration. He moves from gazing to foreplay at this point.

Your temples behind your veil are like the halves of a pome-
granate. Your neck is like the tower of David, built with
elegance; on it hang a thousand shields, all of them shields
of warriors (4:3-4).

Her temples like pomegranates show she had rosy cheeks. Her
neck like a tower explained that he noticed her queenly and erect
posture. References to the shield gives the idea that he looked to her
for strength.

Your two breasts are like two fawns, like twin fawns of a
gazelle that browse among the lilies (4:5).

The reference to her breasts can be better understood by knowing more about gazelles. They are delicate animals, soft to touch and
two-toned, a very white and a darker brown. They are frolicsome
and playful yet graceful and quiet. They were also served to kings as
delicacies. With this in mind, Solomon was probably delighting in
touching and kissing while he admired her form. In Proverbs 5:18-
19, Solomon writes wise words of advice: "Rejoice in the wife of your
youth...May her breasts satisfy you always, may you ever be captivated
by her love."

Because men can find this area of a woman's body playful yet calming, a variety of moods can be experienced while enjoying lovemaking.
Solomon does not rush the process but continues the foreplay. "Until
the day breaks and the shadows flee, I will go to the mountain of
myrrh and to the hill of incense" (Song of Songs 4:6).

This reference can be decoded by other references in this book.
Female genitals are referred to as a garden, and the scents referred to
are frankincense and myrrh.[2] Here, he begins genital foreplay. While
he continues to caress, he continues to verbally express his love also:

All beautiful you are, my darling; there is no flaw in you.
Come with me from Lebanon, my bride, come with me
from Lebanon. Descend from the crest of Amana, from

the top of Senir, the summit of Hermon, from the lions' dens and the mountain haunts of the leopards. You have stolen my heart, my sister, my bride; you have stolen my heart with one glance of your eyes, with one jewel of your necklace. How delightful is your love, my sister, my bride! How much more pleasing is your love than wine, and the fragrance of your perfume than any spice! Your lips drop sweetness as the honeycomb, my bride; milk and honey are under your tongue. The fragrance of your garments is like that of Lebanon (4:7-11).

With descriptions of beautiful places, he tells her that she is stunning. She makes his heart beat faster. Her love is better than wine. Her natural oils, or scent, are better than any scent in nature or made by man. The milk and honey under her tongue tell her that he loves her kisses.

You are a garden locked up, my sister, my bride; you are a spring enclosed, a sealed fountain. Your plants are an orchard of pomegranates with choice fruits, with henna and nard, nard and saffron, calamus and cinnamon, with every kind of incense tree, with myrrh and aloes and all the finest spices (4:12-14).

This is an allusion to her garden again. The fact that he notes the garden was sealed meant she had kept herself for him alone and would not casually give herself to just anyone. All the references to plants were about fragrance-giving plants, so again he is complimenting her naturalness and the scent coming from her arousal as being very pleasing to him. Solomon apparently took his time while lavishing verbal praise and giving physical touch.

Scientific studies have clearly shown that the arousal time is different between men and women.[3] Women take longer to become aroused and relax slower after lovemaking. Men arrive at sexual arousal much quicker. Then, almost immediately after intercourse, they crash into a state of relaxed ecstasy. Solomon was careful to proceed at a rate comfortable to his wife, and he reaped the benefit of fulfilling sex as well. This kind of husband gets a wife who looks forward to lovemaking. No more "I have a headache" jokes. Nope, this lover girl doesn't need Midol or Excedrin when she has an attentive man! She longs to be Solomon's.

> Let him kiss me with the kisses of his mouth—for your love is more delightful than wine. Pleasing is the fragrance of your perfumes; your name is like perfume poured out. No wonder the maidens love you! Take me away with you—let us hurry! Let the king bring me into his chambers (1:2-4).

Did you catch that last line? *She* is saying, "Come here, honey, I'm in a hurry!" His kisses taste better than wine. He is the king—she can have the best wine, and still he is better! His fragrance is better than the best perfume. He can afford personalized Chanel and the best of the fragrances from the outer edges of the exotic realms, and still she says he smells better. Then she gives the ultimate male ego compliment, "All the women love you, but I am yours. Take me!" Then she grabs his hand and pulls him into bed. She is ready!

Your Love Needs Do-Overs

But as with all intimate relationships, this couple's attempts to seduce one another do not always go smoothly. On the heels of a great time together, we see that the Shulammite can be fickle. Maybe it was PMS. Maybe one of her girlfriends whispered some cutting remark. Maybe she was upset over some decision. Or maybe she was just ticked that the king's duties took his attention, but one night when the king came knocking, she did not respond well.

> Open to me, my sister, my darling, my dove, my flawless one. My head is drenched with dew, my hair with the dampness of the night (5:2).

He knocked and expressed his passion. To get to her quarters, the king had to cross a courtyard that took him outside. As a result, his head got covered with the dew from the night air. He, the king, put himself out. He came all this way to make love to his bride, and she responded with an attitude! "I have taken off my robe—must I put it on again? I have washed my feet—must I soil them again?" (5:3).

She was already in bed and did not want to be put out. She might have been tired, or she might not have been in the mood, but either way, she clearly didn't want to be inconvenienced. Her chamber had no central heating, and she had already taken off her robe and was under the covers. The floor was probably dirt, and she may have been thinking, "I just washed my pretty little toes, and he wants me to walk across this dirty floor to open the door! I don't think so!"

Then she starts to realize her mistake as she sees him try to open the door himself. He has a great desire for her, so he gives it one more try. In frustration, he finally gives up and walks away. About that time, her heart pounds for him as she realizes this is exactly the kind of interest she wants him to show her. In a rush of desire, she runs across the floor to open the door for him.

> My lover thrust his hand through the latch-opening; my heart began to pound for him. I arose to open for my lover, and my hands dripped with myrrh, my fingers with flowing myrrh, on the handles of the lock. I opened for my lover, but my lover had left; he was gone. My heart sank at his departure (5:4-6).

All couples experience moments like these. You think tonight is going to be one of your great nights together. You dream of the memories you will develop in your relationship because of the thrill that's on the way. Then it crashes and burns. Disappointment overruns passion. We have good news, though. Life is fitted with do-overs. We have been given an inextinguishable sex drive. We are all wired with an intense desire to love and be loved. Therefore, a breakthrough can happen in your relationship at any time. The desire to be together can be ignited instantly.

Once the Shulammite realizes she is going to miss out on a great time with her lover, she changes her mind, gets up, and finds he has left myrrh on the door handle. Myrrh was a spice that was considered a sensual aphrodisiac. She goes after him.

> I looked for him but did not find him. I called him but he did not answer. The watchmen found me as they made their rounds in the city. They beat me, they bruised me; they took away my cloak, those watchmen of the walls! O daughters of Jerusalem, I charge you—if you find my lover, what will you tell him? Tell him I am faint with love (5:6-8).

She went looking for him. She searched long and hard. She lost her cloak and her haughty attitude. She was desperate to find him. She decided as she returned to her room to mentally prepare herself to be ready for lovemaking when he did return. She begins to think of him head to toe, meditating on his best qualities:

> My lover is radiant and ruddy, outstanding among ten thousand. His head is purest gold; his hair is wavy and black as a raven. His eyes are like doves by the water streams, washed in milk, mounted like jewels. His cheeks are like beds of spice yielding perfume. His lips are like lilies dripping with myrrh. His arms are rods of gold set with chrysolite. His body is like polished ivory decorated with sapphires. His legs are pillars of marble set on bases of pure gold. His appearance is like Lebanon, choice as its cedars. His mouth is sweetness itself; he is altogether lovely. This is my lover, this is my friend, O daughters of Jerusalem (5:10-16).

She says he is dazzling and ruddy, which means handsome and healthy. She also notes that he is outstanding among men. She comments on his raven black hair and says the locks are like clusters of dates. She moves downward in her mind and remembers his dove-like eyes bathed in milk. This is one symbol of purity perched on another.

His cheeks are like a bed of balsam, and his lips are lilies dripping with myrrh. The balsam probably refers to the custom of perfuming the beard. The lilies are most likely red, and the myrrh refers to his sweet breath often aided by the chewing of herbs.[4]

In her daydream she outlines his body. His arms are rods of gold set with beryl, meaning they are strong and he has transparently pink nails. His abdomen is ivory and inlaid with sapphires. Because of the carved reference, he was most likely fit and firm with muscular definition.

She goes down to his legs of marble set on pillars of gold. The marble segment is most likely the part of the loin where the legs separate, and the pillars are his strong legs. The reference to choice cedars also shows her feelings of valuing his strength and masculinity.

Then she declares her adoration for his mouth of sweetness. She was attracted to him not just for his looks but because of his gentle and kind words. She states very clearly the two reasons she misses him—"This is my lover, this is my friend."

Men rarely confide how much they love to know when their wives miss them sexually and are willing to be playful and pursue them. Usually, the simplest remedy for a wife who has lost the passion for her husband is for her to think about her husband's positive attributes and let him know she wants him. When she focuses on the good characteristics of her husband, sexual assertiveness rises up naturally rather than by some artificial imitation or Hollywood make-believe.

On those rare days when life is a bit slower, I (Pam) can easily long for and pursue Bill because I have spent time quietly admiring him. On other, more hectic days, I have to choose to focus my distracted thoughts on Bill and my desire to be with him.

I wish remembering Bill romantically just came easily and naturally, but I often have to direct my thoughts. I keep his picture on my key chain. I might give a quick "I love you" call to his office.

When changing my clothes, I might pull his suit out of his closet just to smell the remaining fragrance of his cologne. I keep the cards he's given me handy so I can reread one or two. But by far, the best way to prepare my heart to enjoy Bill is to take a quiet minute in the car or at my desk, close my eyes, and remember one of our special intimate moments. When I travel, I sometimes take one of Bill's dress shirts that he has just worn a few hours and sleep in it. It keeps my heart connected to his, and my mind and body is better prepared for reentry. Choosing to set aside my distractions and focus my thoughts on Bill draws my heart to his.

The Gift of Anticipation

In chapter 2 of the Song of Songs, we see this young couple engaging in a romantic game with one another.

> My lover is like a gazelle or a young stag. Look! There he stands behind our wall, gazing through the windows, peering through the lattice. My lover spoke and said to me, "Arise, my darling, my beautiful one, and come with me" (2:9-10).

King Solomon is on his way back from a trip when the Shulammite looks out and sees him on the horizon. In her excitement, she sees him as a gazelle that is bounding over the hills to get to her. But Solomon is a king—a man's man. He doesn't bound! He may sprint, he may run, or he may charge, but he certainly does not bound. But in her anticipation of their reunion, she perceives him as a young stag leaping with joy. When he arrives, he keeps the game going as he darts from one window to another, trying to capture her attention. What is the big event they're about to embark on that elicits this much anticipation? They're going to take a walk! That's it. Spring has arrived, and her parents' farm is in full bloom. Their big date consists of a stroll around the family estate to see the flowers. Their efforts at building anticipation, however, make this event a very memorable time for both of them.

After one of my trips away, I wanted to surprise Bill with something extra special. I had returned right before an evening service began at the church Bill was pastoring. I zipped home and changed into one of his favorite outfits. I wrote down on a three-by-five card my favorite places Bill and I had enjoyed each other sexually. I walked into the church midservice as Bill was moving from the back of the room to the pulpit. I gave him a kiss and slid the card into his pocket. He thought I had just given him an announcement he was supposed to read to the congregation. So he pulled the card out, read it to himself silently (praise God!), and turned a bright shade of red. He then winked at me and delivered the shortest sermon in history!

Solomon and his bride used code words for sexuality to build anticipation. For example, all references to "the garden" are references to the female sex organs. She says, "My lover has gone down to his garden, to the beds of spices, to browse in the gardens and to gather lilies. I am my lover's and my lover is mine; he browses among the lilies" (6:3).

It is as if she is saying, "Honey, you are mine and I am yours. I totally trust you. By all means, take your time; have your way with me. I am relaxed and confident in your love for me."

Code Word for *Love*

We encourage couples to have a code word they use to indicate they are desiring sexual interaction. This is especially helpful after children are born. One couple shared how their code word evolved. They were the parents of a couple of toddlers, and life was a bit stressful. The husband's sister, who was single, volunteered to watch the kids so her brother and sister-in-law could go on a date. The relationship was pretty tense, so most of the date was spent just walking and talking at the local lake. The couple picnicked and then talked through life issues as they fed the ducks.

When they returned to the sister-in-law's to retrieve the children, she asked, "So, how'd it go?"

Her brother said, "It was fine. Good. Thanks."

"Good, huh?" she smiled, and the brother caught that his sister thought *good* meant they had taken the date time for sex. He replied, "We just talked and fed the ducks."

"Fed the ducks, huh?" she smiled.

The dad gathered the children and headed out to the car to meet his wife. After the kids were tucked into bed, he explained that his sister thought *feed the ducks* was a code phrase for sex. She replied, "So, want to go feed the ducks?" For years, this couple has been happily feeding the ducks.

One couple we know buys a candle from every place they travel. When one of them is in the mood, the other person is likely to find all those candles lit! "I'll light the candles" is their code.

Our most recent code word was born out of our book *Men Are Like Waffles—Women Are Like Spaghetti*. To understand the code word, you have to have a small glimpse into the meaning of the book title.

Men are like waffles. Men process life in boxes. A waffle is a collection of boxes separated by walls. The boxes are all separate from each other and make convenient holding places. That is typically how a man processes life. A man's thinking is divided up into boxes that have room for only one issue. The first issue of life goes in the first box, the second goes in the second box, and so on. The typical man spends time in only one box at a time. When a man is at work, he is at work. When he is in the garage tinkering around, he is in the garage tinkering. When he is watching TV, he is simply watching TV. Social scientists call this *compartmentalizing*.

Women are like spaghetti. In contrast to men's wafflelike approach, women process life more like a plate of spaghetti. If you look at a plate of spaghetti, you notice that the individual noodles all touch one another. If you attempted to follow one noodle around the plate, you would intersect a lot of other noodles, and you might even switch to another noodle seamlessly. That is how women face life. Every thought and issue is connected to every other thought and issue in some way. Life is much more of a process for women than it is for men. This is why women are typically better at multitasking than men. A woman can talk on the phone, prepare a meal, make a shopping list, work on the planning for tomorrow's business meeting, give instructions to her children as they are going out to play, and close the door with her foot—all without skipping a beat.

When women are under stress, they like to talk their way through the stress, often jumping from subject to subject. Men, on the other hand, like to go to their favorite boxes to recharge. Most of men's favorite easy boxes are actually shaped like boxes: the TV, the computer screen, the newspaper, the football field, the basketball court, the baseball diamond, the tennis court, the garage, the refrigerator, and the bed! The bed box—the sex box—is kind of like that free square in the center of a bingo card. A husband can get to the sex box from every other square in his waffle!

After we had shared this at one conference, anytime we referred to sex, the audience responded by saying, "Bingo!" During Saturday afternoon's free time, one couple went shopping and brought us back a gift they asked us to open in front of the crowd. A note read, "Born to bingo!" So now at our home, when one of us is feeling amorous we ask, "Want to play some bingo?"

The Gift of Adventure

Song of Songs 2 begins with a walk but ends with the Shulammite confidently seeking an adventure with her spouse. After Solomon's wife spends the day dreaming of her love, she sets a game plan. Because she was the one who pushed him away, now she is the one to pursue.

When he enters, she is dancing. In the Hebrew culture, dancing is always connected with joy. The wife was joyous because her lover and friend was home. Solomon was overjoyed at the welcome. He verbally praises her (this time from the feet up) as she dances. "How beautiful are your sandaled feet, O prince's daughter! Your graceful legs are like jewels, the work of a craftsman's hand" (7:1).

Some commentators believe this might have even been an alluring dance. Because Solomon is listing all of her wonderful physical traits, he might have been up close and personal, and she might also have been undressing to give him a better view. Regardless of the details, she is clearly inviting him in closer. How do you extend the invitation to your spouse? The Song of Songs ends with the Shulammite being very forward:

> May the wine go straight to my lover, flowing gently over lips and teeth. I belong to my lover, and his desire is for me. Come, my lover, let us go to the countryside, let us spend the night in the villages. Let us go early to the vineyards to see if the vines have budded, if their blossoms have opened, and if the pomegranates are in bloom—there I will give you my love. The mandrakes send out their fragrance, and at our door is every delicacy, both new and old, that I have stored up for you, my lover (7:9-13).

She wants to go to the countryside to make love, and she explains that the lovemaking will include both "new and old." She is planning how to include the best experiences of the past along with some new ideas to interest him. This passage expresses her growth as a lover. She has gone from shy, introspective, and focused on herself to adventurous, open to new ideas, and most importantly, more focused on her spouse.

The Song of Songs shows that God gives quite a bit of latitude in a marital sexual relationship. We have found three main guiding principles set the foundation for giving the three gifts of sexual pleasure. The gifts of admiration, anticipation, and adventure function best within these boundaries, which help couples say YES! to each other:

Y Yield to one another. What is done in the bedroom must be agreed upon. Love never forces its own way.

E Extend it in love. It must be done in love. The goal is not simply to perform an act. It is to deepen the relationship.

S Secure it with privacy. Sex is only between you two.

The Bible is clear that sex is to be enjoyed between a husband and a wife. No others and no counterfeits (such as porn) are allowed.

Romance to the Rescue

If you want to keep your sex sizzling after you complete this study, pick up our book *Red-Hot Monogamy* (Harvest House), which includes more than 200 red-hot romance and sex ideas. *Red-Hot Monogamy* is an eight-week guide to move your sex life to the front burner of life. To keep our sex life a priority, we have found it helpful to plan some of our sexual times together. Once a week on our calendars, we have written RHM (our code for Red Hot Monogamy), so if someone asks for an appointment, we can honestly say, "Sorry, I have a previous engagement. No one but you two have to know the engagement is for RHM!

One of the previous-engagement ideas to keep sex sizzling is to create theme dates. Pam loves themed dates. Some of our readers and audiences seem to as well. One man wanted to comfort his wife when her parents divorced, so he took her out on a date where the theme was *Always*. He filled the living room with helium balloons, and on the bottom of each was the word *Always*. Over dinner he gave her an inscribed bracelet with the word *Always* on the front. On the back he had inscribed their wedding date and "Till death do us part." He danced with her to the song "Always and Forever," and they watched the movie *Always*. By the end of the night she was sure he would always be there for her.

Another man created a thank-you date where he and his wife relived some of the best moments of their marriage. With each part of the date, he gave her a thank-you card with a puzzle piece inside. As the date progressed, the puzzle was a picture of a hot-air balloon. The last thank-you contained the directions to a field where a hot-air balloon awaited them. The words "Your love lifted me higher" were penned on the card.

We often encourage couples in crisis to revisit their firsts: the first place you said, "I love you," the place you first kissed, the place you had your first date, the place you honeymooned. Nothing is more effective in sparking your love again than to realize what you have invested in the relationship. Having a date of firsts ensures you this won't be your last!

Then there's the "Yahoo! Do I love you!" getaway our sister-in-law gave Pam's brother, Bret, as a birthday present. Bret is a real cowboy. He doesn't simply dress the part; he actually ropes, brands, and drives cattle, but only on the weekends. During the week, he works in the oil industry, but his dream is to one day own a ranch and be a full-time rancher. As a gift to her midlife man, his wife took him to the national rodeo finals. They wore boots and shopped in all the cowboy booths. They ate down-home food every night and listened to country music on the radio.

Pam created a "Let me take you away" date when we were under a huge amount of stress. Our most relaxing vacation had been to Kauai, and we had longed to go back. Neither time, nor life circumstances, nor our checkbook were cooperating, so Pam brought the islands to me. While there the first time, she made note of Hilo Hattie's address, and she ordered some lotions and cocoa butter for a nice massage. She had purchased some island music for $4.99 at a Wal-Mart sale. She borrowed some plants and laid out beach towels in the living room. Then she put on her swimsuit and sarong, and we had a luau!

Another time, Pam had to travel to Japan to speak to leaders, pastor's wives, and missionaries, so while she was there she gathered up the makings for a dream date, Tokyo style. She brought home traditional Japanese music, a Japanese paper lantern, and a set of his and hers kimonos. She greeted me in the airport by placing a Japanese coin in my front trouser pocket and whispered in my ear, "Have I got a *yen* for you!"

One date, Pam wanted to thank me for putting her through college (she took a break from school during my undergraduate and graduate education and while we started our family). On the "You are my hero" date, she gave me gifts of all my favorite things. She wrote a feature article, complete with a picture, titled "World's Best Lover Named." (You'll never see that article in print because it hangs in the privacy of our bedroom.) She gave me my own star on our walk of fame. (Inside the star was a tie tac with the word that I am known for saying when I am preaching or teaching and I come across something I get excited about: "Wow!"

But by far, our most memorable romantic date was one that was almost a complete disaster. It certainly didn't start out a disaster. I received a card in the mail that said, "Our love was made in heaven! Can't wait to see you tonight!" I came home and all the kids had mysteriously vanished. Pam had arranged for them to spend the night at friends. That was unusual for a midweek night. Pam appeared in a new nightie and then sat me on the sofa. She gave me some of my favorite snacks and some coffee. Then she disappeared with, "I'll be back in a moment to get you" as she floated sensually into our room.

Well, "a moment" became quite a long while. This would either be the most exciting surprise I had ever experienced thus far in our relationship, or something had gone very awry. As time ticked by, I began to debate how I should handle this: *Do I go into our room and risk messing up some surprise Pam has dreamed up for us? No—too high a risk of ruining the mood. How long do I stay here? If I don't go in and see if I can help, will she think I'm lazy and insensitive as I sit here eating chocolate and drinking my coffee?* Fortunately, as I debated these no-win options in my mind, Pam emerged from our room. I could see candlelight and hear romantic music. Pam looked as terrific as when she entered 30 minutes before, but on her face I read discouragement and disappointment. Not the look you want to see at the beginning of an intimate rendezvous!

She lifted me up and led me into our room. As we entered I could hear an unusual popping and sizzling noise. In the dim light I looked around and spotted several pans of dry ice and water around our room. Instantly I knew what Pam was trying to do. She was attempting to make a cloud (heaven!) in our room.

I said, "Angel (that really is the pet name I gave her long before this 'heaven' incident), I think I know how to fix this problem."

With a sparkle in her eye, she gave me a big kiss, and then planted herself on the bed with an "I sure hope so!" *Me too!* I thought. I was highly motivated to receive any romantic gift that Pam had taken days to plan! I moved all the remaining dry ice to the sink in our master bedroom. I then put the stopper in the bottom and filled the sink with hot water. I left the hot water running slowly so it leaked out of the overflow. Amazingly, a cloud began to appear and rolled across our floor until it filled our room as high as the bed. We spent the night in heaven!

We enjoyed a perfect romantic encounter as Pam was able to use her amazing creativity and I was able to be the hero and fix the problem, to which she was expressively grateful!

One night after a particularly meaningful sexual encounter, I (Pam) climbed out of bed to pen a poem that Bill found the next day on his mirror:

You're the Winner!
No contest!
No holds barred!
Hands down,
Through the goalposts,
Out of the ballpark,
Nothing but net,
Checkered flag,
Gold medal,
Got my heart,
Winner!

You too have a love made in heaven. Be an angel and give the gifts of admiration, anticipation, and adventure, and you will discover just how heavenly sex was meant to be! You'll both feel like winners then!

Often the remedy to sexual disinterest or dysfunction is to create a loving and accepting environment through kind communication. Even in the case of a medical complication, solutions come easier in an accepting environment. Try one of these exercises to create a more pleasurable atmosphere for lovemaking:

The gift of admiration. Over the next few days, prepare "gifts of praise" designed to encourage each other in the area of insecurity. A few days later, at a predetermined date night, give your gifts of praise to each other. For example, if the wife feels inadequate about her breast size, the husband could center his lovemaking around the breasts, caressing and complimenting while making love. Or if a husband is losing confidence because of difficulty in maintaining an erection or having a slow ejaculation, the wife can simply focus on caressing and kissing all of her husband's body. Her focus also should be on her appreciation of him as a person. She could connect physical and emotional attributes like this, "I love your strong hands. They remind me of how safe I feel when I am being held in your arms."

The gift of anticipation. Read Song of Songs together. Or use Solomon and the Shulammite's example of praising each other from head to toe. Give the gift of encouraging words that will set the tone for anticipating lovemaking. Or select a code word that you can whisper when you are interested.

The gift of adventure. Talk about what you like and what you'd like to try over the next few months. Toss out your ideas, but don't make them a list of expectations. Give your spouse freedom to tuck the idea away and surprise you with it—or not to use it at all. Share the ideas in a brainstorming session and then trust your spouse in his or her timing and implementation.

How to Obtain Golfing Permission

Four married guys went golfing. During the fourth hole, the following conversation took place:

First guy: "You have no idea what I had to do to be able to come golfing this weekend. I had to promise my wife that I'll paint every room in the house next weekend."

Second guy: "That's nothing. I had to promise my wife that I'll build her a new deck for the pool."

Third guy: "Man, you both have it easy! I had to promise my wife that I will remodel the kitchen for her."

As they continued to play the hole, the fourth guy didn't say a word. Finally the others asked him, "You haven't said anything about what you had to do to be able to come golfing this weekend. What's the deal?"

Fourth guy: "I just set my alarm for five thirty a.m. When it went off, I shut off my alarm, gave my wife a nudge, and said, 'Golf course or intercourse?' She just said, 'Wear your sweater.'"

Decide to Discover Your Spouse's Life Motivation

Love is not easily angered.

To be happy with a man, you must understand him a lot and love him a little. To be happy with a woman, you must love her a lot and try not to understand her at all.

I (Pam) love this chapter! It makes me feel the way I do when I find a new shoe store with everything on sale! I feel as if I'm inside a candy store or browsing through a bookstore or a Hallmark shop. This chapter is filled with lots of ideas.

This chapter would not have turned out the way it did if Bill had written it. He is concerned it may be too shallow, like the abridged version of a book. He think it's "CliffsNotes for Relationships."

And that's exactly why I love it! This chapter is "CliffsNotes on Love." It's a sampling of a lot of great information that gives you choices. This information is user-friendly yet profound. It is simple enough that you can apply the information immediately. At the same time, it is profound enough that you can invest in the resources listed in each section of the chapter and study them the rest of your life.

Every summer when I was growing up, I spent time reading the Reader's Digest condensed versions of popular books. Okay, so I'm not going to go to Harvard Law School doing that, but how many of us need to go to Harvard Law School? All we need are a few tools that we can pull out and use when we need them, right?

Think of this chapter as a garage. It holds a collection of tools to help you discover more about your mate. These tools affect your motivation level and effectiveness for expressing your love. When you experience a lull in your relationship, you can pull out one of these tools and add energy back into your home. The tools are listed in rapid-fire succession with quick, simple applications.

I'd Do Anything for You

We were told a precious story of a couple who has been in love a lifetime. The man is always looking for ways to surprise his wife because he knows she loves surprises. Every time he surprises her, she seems to fall more in love with him. Their daughter, with delight and affection, told their story of love:

> Last year Dad decided to get a computer for Mom for Christmas. Knowing very little about computers, Dad contacted a well-known computer supplier when he came across an advertisement for a full setup at a great price.
>
> To keep the gift a surprise, Dad asked to have the computer delivered to the work address of my sister Cindy. You'd think this was not an unusual request, especially around Christmas and with their great deal going on. After over an hour on the phone, my dad hung up only to notice the delivery address he'd provided was slightly different from the address he had written down for Cindy's work. Not one to enjoy talking on the phone, my dear dad reluctantly got back on the phone to correct the delivery address. The Customer Service rep was very helpful and said, "No problem."
>
> Two days later a printer arrived at my parent's house when my mom was home. Dad had no idea they were even getting a printer with the deal and did his best to explain away the strange delivery to my mom.
>
> Within the week (such speedy delivery service!), the balance of the computer arrived on a Thursday—at my

parents' house. This time Mom actually answered the door as Dad was out in the backyard doing some gardening. She freaked. "Oh no, you can't deliver this here. I'm not supposed to see this. Take it away!"

The delivery person calmly responded, "I'm sorry, Ma'am, but this is the delivery address on the package. I have to deliver it here."

Mom signed for what she now knew was her Christmas present. She was now in the possession of two large, fairly heavy boxes that she wasn't supposed to know about. Mom's brain was whirring, trying to think of how she could keep Dad from knowing she knew.

Mom quickly ran next door to their new neighbor, a little old lady with white hair, and explained her predicament. The lady was in stitches and was thrilled to be a part of this escapade. She giggled, "I'd love to help," when Mom requested to bring the boxes over. She agreed to store the boxes in her garage until my sister could pick them up. Cindy was scheduled to come over Tuesday night for her weekly visit. Mom flew to the garage to get their little dolly and wrestled the two secret boxes onto it. With the boxes safely hidden away in the neighbor's garage, Mom called Cindy to let her know what happened. They both agreed she would pick up the boxes when she came to visit Tuesday.

Cindy arrived for her Tuesday visit and went right over to the neighbor, who was still grinning with amusement at our comedy of errors. Once the computer boxes were loaded in the backseat, my sister remembered that Mom and Dad, without fail, walk us out to our cars to wave goodbye when we leave. The boxes were in plain sight in her backseat, so she borrowed a blanket from the little white-haired lady next door to cover the boxes. More giggles! Mom, Dad, and Cindy had a nice visit, and while Mom was out of the room, my sister leaned over and told Dad, "The computer arrived today. I have it in my car."

Dad said, "I already talked with our neighbor. She said we can hide it in her garage. I'll distract Mom while you move the boxes."

Why did they do that? Obviously they love each other. But you might look at your mate and wonder, *Why did he do that?* or *Why did she do that?* How can you build a love life that lasts?

Motivational Tools

Let's look at some relational tools that can keep you and your spouse motivated. These are the power tools of life. When you turn them on, power surges through your spouse's heart, and the willingness to invest in your relationship grows. They are necessary because life requires a lot of energy. It places constant demands on your time and talents. When these demands line up with your natural motivation, stress remains at appropriate levels, and your effectiveness is maximized. But when you are not naturally motivated to meet these demands, stress rises and your effectiveness diminishes. The more you are naturally motivated, the more satisfied you will be with your relationship. These are some of your natural motivational tools:

- temperament style
- conflict resolution style
- learning style
- love language
- birth order
- relax and recharge style
- spiritual gift

We will look at each of these tools a little closer.

Temperament Style

Your temperament determines the way you process the information of life. You discover your temperament by asking two strategic questions: "Am I more extroverted or introverted?" and "Am I more people-oriented or task-oriented?"

Introverts look at life from the inside out. They ask questions like these: "Do I feel emotionally connected to you?" "Does this career make me feel fulfilled?" "Do I feel close to God?" Introverts think before they speak. Sometimes they think long and hard.

Extroverts look at life from the outside in. They ask, "Am I spending enough time at work to climb the ladder?" "Am I spending enough time on my priorities?" "Am I doing the things that will build my relationships?" Extroverts tend to share whatever comes across their mind, so don't panic, they are just thinking out loud! Do you look at life from the outside in (extrovert) or from the inside out (introvert)?

Task-oriented individuals are very good at getting things done. Given the opportunity to spend time with people or finish a task, they will work on the task at hand with the thought, *Everyone will be better when we get done with this.* People-oriented individuals are very good at spending time with people. They can get things done, but they are easily distracted when people walk by because they sincerely want to know what is going on with these people. They believe that everything will get done when everyone is getting along.

Combining the answers to these two questions provides four distinct temperament types as we see in the chart on the next page.

Originally, the temperaments were referred to as sanguine, choleric, melancholy, and phlegmatic. On the chart, we have listed several resources and what each author might call the personality types. Study one of the many resources listed and have every member of your family take the fun temperament quizzes to discern his or her personality type. We will base our discussion on some easy-to-remember terms used by Florence Littauer:

PEOPLE-ORIENTED	TASK-ORIENTED	

PERSONALITY TYPE I
POPULAR
Sanguine

Motivated by:
ATTENTION

Brawner: Otter
Phillips: Expressive
DISC: Inspirational
Littauer: Yellow like the sun
Biblical Example: John the Baptist

PERSONALITY TYPE II
POWERFUL
Choleric

Motivated by:
Being in CONTROL

Brawner: Lion
Phillips: Driver
DISC: Dominant
Littauer: Red like fire
Biblical Example: Peter

PERSONALITY TYPE III
PEACEFUL
Phlegmatic

Motivated by:
RESPECT & ACCEPTANCE

Brawner: Retriever
Phillips: Amiable
DISC: Steady
Littauer: Green like grass
Biblical Example: Barnabas

PERSONALITY TYPE IV
PERFECT
Melancholy

Motivated by:
ANSWERS & STRUCTURE

Brawner: Beaver
Phillips: Analytical
DISC: Cautious
Littauer: Blue like the ocean
Biblical Example: Martha

EXTROVERT

INTROVERT

- popular (sanguine)
- powerful (choleric)
- perfect (melancholy)
- peaceful (phlegmatic)

When taking a personality profile as an adult, try to think back to what you were like as a child of seven or eight. Often, as adults we have learned to mask our true self in order to please other people. Or, more positively, we have gained the skills to strengthen our perceived weaknesses with a goal of becoming more like Jesus. (Jesus would, of course, have all the strengths of all the personalities and none of the weaknesses!)

The powerful. Cholerics are extroverted, task-oriented, decision-makers, and natural leaders. Bob Phillips, in his book *The Delicate Art of Dancing with Porcupines,* labels them *drivers* and the DISC profile test uses the word *dominant.* Their primary shortcomings are a lack of empathy and a bulldozer mentality. They are focused on the task at hand, so they can sometimes run over people to get it done. They are primarily motivated by power. Fun to them is anything they decide on. The best way to motivate a choleric is to give him or her choices. This powerful personality loves to be the leader or boss. Without these powerful personalities, the world might just stop because they are the driving force behind most great goals and dreams. Other people may dream great dreams, but cholerics wake up and make them happen!

The popular. The other extrovert is the people-oriented sanguine. In *Taming the Family Zoo,* Jim and Suzette Brawner label these people *otters* because they love to have fun. Phillips calls them *expressive,* the DISC, *inspirational.* They are creative, spontaneous, and have super people skills! Their primary weakness is a lack of perseverance. (If it isn't fun, why stay at it?) They love a party, so they can seem shallow and flippant to some of the other personalities. They are primarily motivated by people and praise. All they want is a little attention—okay, a lot of attention—and they will do anything to get it. If you want to motivate sanguines, hook a task to a person or make it a party, and they are there for you! Without these popular personalities, many of us would have fewer friends. The popular personalities make the world a tolerable, happy place to dwell.

The peaceful. The phlegmatic, or the Brawner's *retriever,* is an introverted, amiable, steady, no-frills, peace-at-all costs, likeable guy or gal. Phillips labels these as *amiable;* the DISC says they are *steady.* Everybody loves the peaceful personality. Everyone gets along with them because their goal in life is not to rock the boat. Everyone likes retrievers unless you want something done, you need a decision out of them, or you are in a hurry. Then they can drive you crazy!

I am married to a man whose secondary personality is peaceful. All that a peaceful personality needs in life is to be appreciated. I know I could not do what I do as a leader, traveling speaker, and writer if Bill weren't in my life. He really is the wind beneath my wings. Even while writing this book, I told him, "Honey, I need you. You are my inspiration," and I meant it. People just function better with a little TLC, and the peaceful personalities can give emotional support well.

The theme song of the peaceful personality would be Aretha Franklin's "Respect"! All they want is a little respect. When you show appreciation and respect to these people, they will do almost anything for you. They might take a while, but they will get it done. Most of us just couldn't get along without these natural mediators.

The perfect. This melancholy personality is introverted and task-oriented. Most great artists and musicians are this personality. They are creative, and they want things done right. They have the patience to do things with excellence. Their perfectionism can drive other people, primarily the sanguine, crazy. The sanguine's response to a melancholy will always be, "lighten up!" But they can't lighten up. The world is black-and-white and is in desperate need of fixing to these folks. They can become negative and depressed because they see the glass half-empty, and they notice all the little undone things in the world.

The Brawners' model calls these people *beavers* because they are hardworking and get the job done. The DISC test calls them *cautious,* and Bob Phillips labels them as *analytical.* They are always thinking, processing.

Since I am sanguine and choleric, I can create ideas in bucketfuls, and I of course think all of them are brilliant because I came up with them. I want to set sail with a host of ideas. Bill is my rudder in life, helping me to sort through the ideas, choose the best ones, and make them rise to the level of excellence. Without him, my impatience would cause me to make many mistakes—possibly a few tragic ones.

So if you are married to a perfect personality, make very few promises, or you will lose credibility. If you say you are going to be home at six p.m., you'd better do it. If you come in at 6:20, you weren't late—you lied. The perfect personality takes everything very literally. Without the perfect personality, the world would be filled with so many more mistakes. Imagine the perfects as those who set all the synchronized traffic lights. Chaos would happen without them!

Resources for Further Study

Brawner, Jim, and Suzette Brawner. *Taming the Family Zoo.* NavPress, 1998.

The DISC Profile. www.discprofile.com or www.onlinedisc.com.

Littauer, Florence. *Personality Plus.* Fleming H. Revell Company, 1992.

Phillips, Bob. *The Delicate Art of Dancing with Porcupines.* Gospel Light Publications, 1989.

Trent, John, Rodney Cox, and Eric Tooker. *Leading from Your Strengths.* Broadman & Holman Publishers, 2004.

Conflict Resolution Style

Stress and conflict bring out different things in different people, and you do well to know how your mate tends to solve problems. Once you know his or her bent, you can work with it to create a pattern that is workable for the two of you to get to resolution. In chapter 4 we listed several conflict resolution styles. Which are you? Which is your mate?

- negotiators
- debaters
- peacekeepers
- drama team
- survivors
- servants

Resources for Further Study

Gottman, John. *Why Marriages Succeed or Fail.* Simon & Schuster Adult Publishing Group, 1995.

Gottman, John, and Nan Silver. *Seven Principles for Making Marriage Work.* Crown Publishing Group, 2000.

Learning Style

Cynthia Tobias, in her book *The Way They Learn,* describes how people process information:

- Auditory learners remember information best if they hear it.
- Visual learners remember best if they have seen the information.
- Kinesthetic learners learn by experience or touch.

You might think this isn't important if you are out of school, but wait until you need to make an important decision. One of you might need to access information on charts and the other might need books on tape to make the decision.

Resources for Further Study

Tobias, Cynthia. *The Way They Learn.* Tyndale House Publishers, 1996.

Love Language

We highly recommend Gary Chapman's *The Five Love Languages.* All the expressions of love listed below can be effective, but each of us has a favorite way to receive love from our spouse. If you had to choose, which would be your favorite way for your mate to express his or her love toward you?

- words of affirmation
- physical touch
- quality time
- acts of service
- gifts

Resources for Further Study

Chapman, Gary. *The Five Love Languages.* Moody Publishers, 1996.

Chapman, Gary, and Ross Campbell. *The Five Love Languages of Children.* Moody Publishers, 1997.

Birth Order

Your placement in the family you grew up in impacted who you are today. Dr. Kevin Leman, in *The New Birth Order Book,* offers a short sample quiz to help the reader get a quick grasp of birth order:

> Which of the following sets of personality traits fits you best?
>
> A. Perfectionist, reliable, conscientious, list maker, well organized, hard-driving, natural leader, critical, serious, scholarly, logical, doesn't like surprises, loves computers.
>
> B. Mediator, compromising, diplomatic, avoids conflict, independent, loyal to peers, many friends, a maverick, secretive, unspoiled.

C. Manipulative, charming, blames others, attention seeker, tenacious, people person, natural salesperson, precocious, engaging, affectionate, loves surprises.

D. Little adult by age seven, very thorough, deliberate, high achiever, self-motivated, fearful, cautious, voracious reader, black-and-white thinker, uses "very," "extremely," and "exactly" a lot, can't bear to fail, has very high expectations for self, more comfortable with people who are older or younger.

If you noted that the test seemed rather easy because A, B, and C listed traits of the oldest right on down to the youngest in the family, you are right. If you picked list A, it's a very good bet you are firstborn in your family. If you chose list B, chances are you are a middle child...If list C seemed to relate best to who you are, it's likely you are the baby in the family...But what about list D? It describes the only child.

It is interesting to note that two middle children have the best odds at long-term love because they are trained to negotiate and compromise as part of the family dynamic. Two firstborns need lots of relational training because they will both want to be in charge.

Resources for Further Study

Leman, Kevin. *The New Birth Order Book.* Fleming H. Revell Company, 1998.

Relax and Recharge Style

- *Busy bee.* Even on vacation this person has a to-do list. He or she comes into a vacation or day off with a schedule and plan.

- *Social butterfly.* These people believe vacations are all about relationship, so driving two days each way on a five-day trip is just fine if they can see their relatives.

- *Waiting walking stick.* These people like to sit still on vacation or a day off. Give them a hammock and a book, and they are happy.
- *Active ant.* These people enjoy activities and athletics on their days off. You'll find them jetskiing, kayaking, snowboarding, hiking, and the like.
- *Luggage ladybug.* These people prefer guided tours, group outings, and professionals in charge of their free time.

If you talk through your downtime, keeping your style in mind, less of free time will be used for arguments and more of it used for fun activities!

Resources for Further Study

Farrel, Bill, and Pam Farrel. *Men Are Like Waffles—Women Are Like Spaghetti.* Harvest House Publishers, 2001.

Spiritual Gifts

I fell in love with Bill because he was so compassionate. However, I soon found that his compassion applied to all of humankind! People who are in distress seek out Bill because he is a gifted people helper. If we are walking down a crowded city street and a homeless person sees us approach, he or she will *always* talk to Bill and ask for help. If Bill is with a group of men and someone's car has a flat or he has locked his keys in his car, the person will *always* ask Bill for help. This is so predictable, it has become comical.

Once, when leaving for an anniversary vacation in Hawaii, I bought Bill a T-shirt that read, "Witness Protection Program: You don't know me!" It still didn't help. Even then people in need approached him.

He turned to me and asked, "What is it with me? Why do I always look like the one who can solve a person's problem?"

I smiled and said, "Might be the superman cape sticking out from under your shirt."

Then it hit me. That had been my nickname for Bill nearly all our married life: Superman. I had seen it when I was a 20-year-old, and I adored it. At times when we are on a family trip and his cell phone rings with a crisis on the other end, I get frustrated or even angry. I think to myself, *Why does the whole world need him? Can't their problems wait just one day while we spend time together?*

Over the years, we had to learn to make compromises. I learned that having to share Bill with the world is a small price to pay to be married to a man with his amazing heart and character. He learned to set up boundaries and protect days off, holidays, and vacations. He decided to meet people only at the office so our home could be a place of rest and family connection.

We should make room for one another's gifts instead of being frustrated by them. For example, a couple can become frustrated if the wife has the gift of hospitality and the husband is the kind of person who doesn't like many people around or doesn't want people to mess with his stuff. Can you see how a situation like this might cause some anxiety even though it involves your area of strength?

These gifts are God-given and enhance your life in a powerful way. They are also so powerful that they can disrupt your life if they run unchecked. A couple can come to a place of agreement by being aware of each other's gifts and making allowances for them. Consider a couple who is asked to teach together. If he has the gift of teaching but she has the gift of helps, he could teach and she could handle hospitality, provide resources, and make phone calls. She can be available for individual discussions to help people apply the material to their lives while staying in the background. This gives them both the opportunity to work in their comfort range.

The social butterfly married to the king of the castle might compromise and create a home that is guest friendly but includes a private space that is off-limits to company. That way, he can retreat if the company chaos becomes too much for him.

Talk with your mate about the list below. This is not an exhaustive list of gifts but rather a place to begin the dialogue. Discuss how you can make room for each other's gifts, and find creative solutions for any differences.

- Administration: directing projects (Romans 12:8; 1 Corinthians 12:5,28).

- Craftsmanship and artistry: using your hands to create or build so that others are pointed toward God (Exodus 30:22-25; 2 Chronicles 34:9-13; Acts 16:14; 18:3).

- Evangelism: communicating spiritual truth to lead someone to a personal relationship with God (Acts 5:42; Romans 10:15; Ephesians 4:11; 2 Timothy 4:5).

- Exhortation: encouraging people and walking alongside them to bring out the best in them (Romans 12:8; 1 Corinthians 2:1-2; 2 Corinthians 9:2).

- Giving: providing faithful stewardship and sharing with others (Mark 12:41-44; Luke 18:12; Romans 12:8; 2 Corinthians 8:1-7).

- Helps and serving: caring for others by working behind the scenes (Mark 2:3-4; Luke 22:22-27; Romans 16:1-2; 12:7; 1 Corinthians 12:28; 1 Timothy 6:2; 1 Peter 4:9-10).

- Hospitality: using the home or other resources to make people feel included and welcomed (Acts 16:15; 21:16-17; Romans 12:9-13; 16:23).

- Intercession: devoting time and energy to pray more than the average person does (Acts 12:1-17; 16:25-31; Colossians 4:12; 1 Timothy 2:1-8).

- Knowledge: sharing information that helps people live life in a productive, healthy manner (Romans 15:14; 1 Corinthians 12:8; 13:8).

- Leadership: directing people (1 Timothy 5:17).

- Mercy: showing compassion and acting to meet needs (Luke 10:33-35; Acts 9:36; 16:33-34; Romans 12:8).

- Music: singing or playing instruments to turn hearts toward God (1 Samuel 16:16; 1 Chronicles 16:41-42; 2 Chronicles 5:12-13).

- Prophecy: publicly proclaiming truth (Ezra 6:1; Isaiah 14:28; 20:45; 25:1; 1 Corinthians 12:10; 13:2; 14:1).

- Teaching: explaining harder concepts to others and helping them apply them (Romans 12:7; 1 Corinthians 12:28; Ephesians 4:11; 1 Timothy 3:2).

- Wisdom: applying knowledge with discretion and insight (2 Chronicles 1:11-12; Proverbs 1:2; 2:10).

- Writing: communicating information to help others grow in faith, develop life skills, or turn toward God (Psalm 45:1; Acts 15:19-20; Philippians 3:1; 1 Timothy 3:14-15).

Resources for Further Study

"Team Ministry Spiritual Gift Analysis." www.churchgrowth.org/analysis/index.html.

"Towns Spiritual Gift Questionnaire." www.elmertowns.com/spiritual_gifts_test.

Wagner, C. Peter. *Discover Your Spiritual Gift.* Gospel Light, 2002.

Finesse Tools

Some areas of life are more sensitive than others. These areas require us to develop skills to avoid making mistakes. As your skill grows, your impact increases. If your skills remain underdeveloped, your actions will result in unwelcome consequences and deterioration in your relationship. These tools require practice to develop finesse and proficiency. These finesse tools include your financial style and your parenting style.

Financial Style

My friend Ellie Kay, in *A Woman's Guide to Family Finances*, describes several money-management styles. We've adapted these for both genders and condensed their descriptions. You will notice that most of these styles are reactions to fear or insecurity. The most mature style is one of balance that addresses both the present and the future. It takes hard work and cooperation, and most couples find it to be challenging. A couple that wants to achieve this balance must identify where they are starting from and then set goals to guide their journey. We encourage you to get Ellie's book and learn more, especially if you want to save money or get out of debt!

- Power Paul (or Polly): The person with the money has the power.

- Secure Samantha (or Sam): This born saver feels secure only if she or he saves "just a little more." Fear is an underlying emotion.

- Tightwad Tilly (or Tom): Beyond frugal, this person often holds on to money instead of spending it on relationships.

- Worrywart Wanda (or Ward): This person obsesses about money. He or she is held captive by what-ifs. *What if people only love me for my money? What if I make a bad investment?* He or she thinks about money too much.

- Spendthrift Steve (or Stephanie): If this person has a dollar, he or she needs to spend it!

- Feel good Francine (or Frank): If this person feels bad, off he or she goes to the mall!

- Love ya Louie (or Louise): This person uses money to make people feel good about him or her.

- Balanced Betty (or Bob): This person has good financial habits, and his or her attitudes toward money are balanced and healthy.

Resources for Further Study

Kay, Ellie. *A Woman's Guide to Family Finances*. Bethany House Publishers, 2003.

Parenting Style

You have a parenting style that guides your actions with your children. The way you parent is a combination of what you saw modeled by your parents and what you have decided to learn on your own. Good parenting is not automatic. Parenting is a growing process that you can learn. You can become a better parent than you currently are, or you can deteriorate in your parenting skills. The most effective parenting is proactive but requires a lot of energy and focus to achieve. You can begin to be a proactive parent in the same way that you begin to find financial balance—by identifying your starting point and creating a plan for growth. Which of these styles best describes you?

- Permissive: These parents border on apathy or neglect. They are too busy, too broken, or too self-absorbed to care.

- Popular: These parents are so concerned about maintaining a friendship with the child that they won't risk the friendship by providing rules, boundaries, or discipline.

- Paranoid: These parents worry about everything and make decisions based on fear.

- Prescriptive: These parents wait until issues become problems before they act.

- Proactive: These parents prayerfully set goals, make plans, and discuss parenting choices ahead of time to guide and lead a child forward.

Resources for Further Study

Arp, Dave, and Claudia Arp. *And Suddenly They're Thirteen.* Zondervan, 1999.

Dobson, James. *The New Dare to Discipline.* Tyndale House Publishers, 1996.

————. *The New Strong-Willed Child.* Tyndale House Publishers, 2004.

Farrel, Bill, and Pam Farrel. *The 10 Best Decisons Every Parent Can Make.* Harvest House Publishers, 2001.

So What Now?

Now that we know all these things about ourselves and our spouse, what do we do with the information? We have some choices. We can use it against each other, bringing it up in arguments or manipulating to gain an advantage. Or we can use it to excuse our own unhealthy behaviors. Neither of these is highly effective because God wants us to grow in grace and mature in areas of weakness.

A much more useful approach is to discover each other's strengths and uniqueness. These are the very qualities that caused you to fall in love with each other, so every time you rediscover them you become fascinated with your relationship. If you stay aware of these traits, you can use them to strengthen your relationship.

Bill often tells others he is living a much larger life because he is married to me. He is so easygoing that he would not naturally choose the visionary, idealistic path. He is so people oriented that he would stop all along the way to meet every person he came across.

I am so visionary and idealistic that I can forget to count the costs of decisions ahead of time. I am prone to thinking I can just handle those things as they come along. Because I am so extroverted, I can be tempted to live a shallow life. Because I am married to Bill, I have learned to use my gifts of writing and speaking to share all the wonderful, deep, practical, people-helping information Bill has created. God has formed an unstoppable team. Bill creates materials that are proven to help people, and I package and present them. I envision what can be. Bill ensures our plans are thought through, and then I push them forward by my faith.

The Gift of Acceptance

In order to utilize these tools, you must accept each other. Accepting and celebrating your differences allows each of you to use these traits and affirm each other as a unique creation of God. When I graduated from college, Bill gathered my friends and threw a "This Is Your Life" party. Several of the blondes acted out different stages of my life. I have never laughed so hard as I watched them make a melodrama from all my habits and idiosyncrasies.

When Bill was celebrating his ten-year anniversary as senior pastor, I gathered some friends to celebrate. They created a humorous and poignant drama of all the things Bill could have been if he didn't follow the call to pastoral ministry (coach, counselor, draftsman, or doctor) and how he was using all those skills and talents in his ministry to people. He felt valued and appreciated.

Look for a way to observe your mate and celebrate him or her. What trait can you encourage and appreciate? Romance is nothing more than seeing the masterpiece God has given you in your spouse and taking the time to applaud it. Box up your admiration, tie it with a bow, and give it with your sincere verbal praise. Then sit back and watch the flame of your passion ignite.

Now it's your turn. Open your relational toolbox and identify the resources you can use to build your relationship. How would you describe you and your spouse in each of these areas?

- Personality style:
- Conflict resolution style:
- Learning style:
- Love language:
- Birth order:
- Relax and recharge style:
- Spiritual gift:
- Financial style:
- Parenting style:

What He Says—What He Means

"I'm going fishing."

This really means he's going to stand by a stream with a stick in his hand all day while the fish swim by in complete safety.

"It's a guy thing."

He is acting with no rational thought. Don't even hope for a logical explanation.

"Can I help with dinner?"

He wants to know why it isn't already on the table.

"Uh-huh." "Sure, honey." "Yes, dear."

These mean absolutely nothing. They are conditioned responses.

"It would take too long to explain."

He has no idea how it works.

"We're going to be late."

He thinks he has a legitimate excuse for driving like a maniac.

"Take a break, honey. You're working too hard."

He can't hear the game over the vacuum cleaner.

"That's interesting, dear."

He is wondering why you're still talking.

"Hey, I've got my reasons for what I'm doing."

He is hoping he can think of some pretty soon.

"I can't find it."

It didn't fall into his outstretched hands, so he's completely clueless.

"You know I could never love anyone else."

He realizes it could be worse.

"You look terrific."

He is pleading with you not to try on one more outfit. He's starving.

"I'm not lost. I know exactly where we are."

He's wondering if anyone will ever see you alive again.

Words Women Use

"Fine."

This is the word women use to end an argument when they feel they are right and you need to shut up. Never use "fine" to describe how a woman looks—this will cause you to have one of those arguments.

"Five minutes."

This is half an hour. It is equivalent to the five minutes that your football game is going to last before you take out the trash, so it's an even trade.

"Nothing."

This means "something," and you should be on your toes. "Nothing" is usually used to describe the feeling a woman has of wanting to turn you inside out, upside down, and backward. "Nothing" usually signals the beginning of an argument that will last "five minutes" and end with "fine."

"Go ahead" (with raised eyebrows).

> This is a dare—one that will result in a woman getting upset over "nothing" and will end with "fine."

"Go ahead" (normal eyebrows).

> This means "I give up" or "Do what you want because I don't care." You will get a "raised eyebrow go ahead" in just a few minutes, followed by "nothing" and "fine." She will talk to you in about "five minutes," when she cools off.

(Loud sigh)

> This is not actually a word but a nonverbal statement often misunderstood by men. A loud sigh means she thinks you are an idiot and wonders why she is wasting her time arguing with you over "nothing."

(Soft sigh)

> Again, not a word but a nonverbal statement. Soft sighs mean that she is content. Your best bet is not to move or breathe, and she will stay content.

"That's okay."

> This is one of the most dangerous statements that a woman can make to a man. "That's okay" means that she wants to think long and hard before paying you back for whatever it is that you have done. "That's okay" is often used with a raised-eyebrow "fine."

"Go ahead!"

> At some point in the near future, you are going to be in some mighty big trouble.

"Please do."

> This is not a statement—it is an offer. A woman is giving you the chance to come up with an excuse for doing whatever it is that you have done. You have a fair chance with the truth, so be careful, and you shouldn't get a "That's okay."

"Thanks."

A woman is thanking you. Do not faint. Just say, "You're welcome."

"Thanks a lot."

This is much different from "thanks." A woman will say "Thanks a lot" when she is really ticked off at you. It signifies that you have offended her in some callous way, and it will be followed by a loud sigh. Be careful not to ask what is wrong after the loud sigh—she will only tell you "Nothing."

8

Decide to Tackle Transitions

Love keeps no record of wrongs.

Adam and Eve had an ideal marriage. He didn't have to hear about all the men she could have married, and she didn't have to hear about the way his mother cooked.

One of the great things about having been a pastor for 20 years is that I have been privileged to perform hundreds of weddings. Weddings are generally beautiful affairs with everyone on their best behavior. But sometimes the best part of the wedding is the part that goes wrong!

The biggest mistake I ever made at a wedding was performing an entire ceremony with my zipper down. I was wearing a wireless microphone with an antenna that ran down my pant leg. I went to the bathroom to snake the antenna down my trousers and forgot just one little detail. I performed the ceremony, pronounced the couple husband and wife, and headed backstage to remove the microphone when I noticed the debacle. I debated with myself: *Should I go to the reception or just sneak out the back and go home?* I don't know whether the people were being polite or if they really didn't notice, but nobody mentioned my little addition to the ceremony.

I wanted to make sure this never happened again, so I took extra measures at the next ceremony I performed. It happened to be Pam's sister's wedding. Just before departing the office to walk into the auditorium, I turned to the groom and his attendants and said, "Men, check your flies." I had forgotten that I was wearing two microphones that day. The microphone that was wired into the house system was turned off, but the direct feed into the video camera was on. When Pam's sister got back from her honeymoon, she invited us over for dinner so she could show us the video. During the candlelighting portion of the ceremony, my voice is forever preserved on videotape saying, "Men, check your flies!"

I also had the opportunity to perform the wedding of the original drama queen. It took place in a private backyard under an archway on top of a three-step landing. We were in the middle of her vows when her knees started to buckle. I said to the groom, "You'd better grab her. She's going down." He grabbed onto her arms and escorted her down the three steps. The front row of guests cleared so she could sit down. People thoughtfully fanned her and brought her water. But before she could take her first drink of water, she dry heaved three times with all the accompanying sounds! The whole time, the video was running and following her every move! With a few sips of water and a lot of attention, she miraculously recovered, said to her groom, "Okay, I'm ready to go," and took her place at the altar again. The rest of the ceremony went off without a hitch, but the memory lingers.

Not long ago, I experienced my epic wedding moment. The groom had lived as difficult a life as any I have encountered. His mother died of a drug overdose when he was very young. His father was put in jail about six months later for dealing drugs. He was shuffled between various foster homes before finally being adopted by his grammar school principal. He had assumed he would never get married because he didn't believe that anyone would really love him. Then he met a young lady who fell in love with him and thought he was the greatest thing that ever hit the planet.

He told the men in his wedding party to join him in wearing sunglasses at the outdoor wedding, not because he wanted to look cool but because he knew he was going to cry through the whole ceremony. Sure enough, he was so touched by the love of this woman that he started crying when we lined up to go in. He continued crying as he watched the ladies enter. He cried even more when he first saw his bride. He cried through the entire ceremony!

Someone who cries for that long gets a very runny nose, and he was doing nothing about it. We were approaching the big moment when he would kiss the bride, and he had two big snot beads running down his upper lip. I wasn't sure if I should stop the proceedings and tell him to clean himself up or if I should just let it play out. I decided to just carry on with the ceremony. I pronounced them man and wife and then said to him, "You may now kiss your wife." He reached up with his right hand, wiped the slime off his lip, put his right hand behind her neck and gave her a big kiss! Her lack of complaints was one of the finest displays of unconditional love I have ever seen.

We all head into marriage with the hope that every day will be as happy as our wedding day and that we will live happily ever after. In reality, however, the great moments are mixed with embarrassing, awkward transitions.

Tackle Those Transitions

In more than 25 years of working with couples, we have observed that the transitions in life can make or break a marriage. Ecclesiastes 3 refers to a time and a season for everything, so life comes prepackaged with transitions. These transitions require of us a new level of skill and determination. They change the scenery of our lives and take us to new heights or depths. How you handle these transitions will affect the quality and stability of your marriage. They will challenge you to be stronger people, and they provide opportunities for greater enrichment and enhancement.

Transitions are a bit like dynamite. They have the power to move mountains and create an easier path, but they can also destroy things. The decision is yours. You can allow the transitions to tear you two apart, or you can team up and tackle the transitions together. Sadly, too many people choose to opt out, so that one-quarter of all Americans have experienced at least one divorce.[1]

Although people commonly call it quits, studies are confirming the benefits of hanging in there. Couples who consider divorce but decide not to file rate their personal happiness level five years later higher than those who decided to divorce. And the couples in the greatest conflict show the most marital upswing in their happiness rating![2]

A tornado provides a great picture of how pivotal these transitions can be. In the movie *Twister*, a tornado chases two scientists (a man and a woman). The tornado is destroying everything in its path, and it is after this couple. This is often how we feel in life. Life seems to have us in its sights, pursuing us relentlessly until we are destroyed.

Just minutes from disaster, the two run into a pump house and look around for options. They notice a U-shaped pipe anchored into the ground. They decide to lash themselves together and strap themselves to the pipe. The tornado rips the shed off its foundation and turns the couple upside down. They hover in the air until the tornado passes. If they had not been securely anchored, they would have been lost. Instead, they shared the ride of their lives! That's what transitions do. They either destroy us or bond us. The choice is ours.

You cannot avoid transitions. You must travel through them in order to fully mature in life. If you prepare well for them and find ways to support each other as you go through them, they become a source of connection instead of conflict. Let's consider a few typical transitions and ways we can travel through them to become stronger couples who are more in love each day.

Beginning Bliss

Most couples rate their marital satisfaction high in the first year of marriage. Even though this is a time of adjustment as two lifestyles are merged together, couples have a strong sense of hope. Life is filled with new experiences, and couples generally believe they will work through their difficulties.

You can take steps to increase your satisfaction as you start out together. A random phone survey showed that 35 percent of couples married five years or less had premarital counseling in a religious context, and 75 percent of these couples reported that this preparation was helpful to them.[3] Training can raise your skill level and make you more capable of having an intimate relationship. A marriage enrichment training flier that came across our desk recently showed that couples lower the likelihood of divorce with every premarital counseling session they participate in! Even reading this book is lowering your chances for divorce! Marriage preparation and training are most needed in the early years of marriage. The longer you are married, the more likely you are to stay married. The majority of divorces happen earlier in the marriage rather than later. The chances of those who have been married 35 years divorcing are almost nil.

What can couples do early in their relationship to nurture their love and provide protection for their relationship?

Get Training

We went to our first marriage conference when we'd been married one month. We went at the insistence of some friends at church who recommended United Marriage Encounter because it had saved their 20-year marriage. We thought, *If the skills helped them save their marriage, maybe we can avoid those problems altogether if we get the training!* We were right! We learned a few key tools that weekend that laid a great foundation: Have a weekly date night, have a daily talk time, pray at least once a day, attend church weekly. Many of the items were things we were already doing, but we also learned the value of writing love letters and reading them aloud to each other, a practice we still cherish to this day.

In a Groove (but Not a Rut)

In a terrific message at a recent Smart Marriages conference, William Doherty explained the need and benefits of marriage rituals—those quaint habits that draw two hearts closer:

> We fall in love through rituals of connection and intimacy—courtship rituals like romantic dinners, long talks, riding bicycles or going skiing, going for walks,

exchanging gifts, talking every night on the telephone. We mostly do these rituals alone as a couple—when people are falling in love, their family and friends know to give them some space. We gladly fill our time through rituals of connection and intimacy. We develop a common language and a common experience bank. We go to dinner at our favorite spots, and we try to sit at our favorite tables. We go dancing at our favorite places...

[A friend] told me about the mundane activity she and her husband do every Saturday that helps her feel close to him: They do errands. For them, this is a ritual of connection. You see, if they did their shopping efficiently, they would divide up, right? Rituals are not efficient; they are about connection. So my friend and her husband do errands together and talk along the way. I bash TV all the time, but I know a couple who, when they watch a favorite TV show, sometimes take turns giving each other a shoulder rub, with one sitting on the floor and the other on the couch...Almost anything can be turned into a ritual of connection, if the focus is on the relationship.[4]

Early in relationships, rituals are almost natural. We meet, we greet, we kiss, we say, "I love you. How was your day?" But couples can drift from the rituals that built their relationship if they are not careful. Doherty continues:

I once asked a couple I was seeing in therapy about their greeting ritual. The wife was usually home, in the kitchen. The four children and the golden retriever were somewhere in the house. This is what would happen: The husband walks in, greeted first by the dog with a big, enthusiastic show of affection. Dogs are great ritualists; they are consistent, they are loving, they are excited to see you. You can actually chart the number of hours you've been gone, and correlate that with the energy of their greeting ritual. So, the husband walks in the door, is greeted by the golden retriever, and next by the kids, with hugs all around for child one, two, three, and four. And then he goes to the bedroom and changes clothes. His wife remains in the kitchen. Some time over the next 20 minutes he wanders into the kitchen and the first words uttered by one or the other are something like, "Jesse has a concert tonight, so we have to speed up dinner." I asked this couple how they greeted each other when they were newlyweds. With sheepish grins, they recounted that it was "Hi, honey, how are you?" Followed by huggy, kissy, and "How was your day?" I asked them if they remembered when that changed. Not a clue. Most of us are clueless about the decline in our marital rituals.

Here is the talk ritual in my marriage. This is one that Leah and I came up with when our youngest child was four. After dinner, we would clean up, give the kids dessert, one of us would start the coffee, and then we told our children to go play. We taught them to leave us in peace while we had our coffee, so that we could talk. We said basically to not interrupt us unless the house is burning or something equivalent, in which case they can always call 911 and then interrupt us…So we had about fifteen minutes every day to talk as a couple.

This daily conversation has the three phases of a ritual. *First, a clear transition.* Anthropologists refer to this as the transition to ritual space. It simply doesn't work to say, "Let's just find fifteen minutes every evening." When?…Set a specific time, say, eight thirty till a quarter of nine?…It simply doesn't work unless you have a clear, regular transition point that is calibrated to some event. And so for us, the time was dinner, followed by coffee. Of course, if one of us had to leave immediately after dinner, we did not have the talk rituals, but we always noted the exception. One of the ways you know you have a solid ritual is that, when you cannot do it for some reason, you make mention of that fact…

The second is the enactment phase, when you are actually engaged in the ritual activity, in this case a conversation. Here Leah and I evolved some ground rules. No logistics talk. No talk about getting the lawn mowed or the electric bill paid. No problem-solving talk. No conflict items: "Now that I've got your attention, let me tell you how upset I am about what you said last night." If you do logistical talk, you will not connect at a personal level, so why do the ritual? And if you let conflict and problem solving enter the conversation, then one or both of you is likely to start avoiding the talk ritual because you may not feel up to working so hard on your relationship. In fact, a general ground rule for all family rituals is keep conflict out if at all possible. If you go out on a date, do not bring up unpleasant topics. Do not discuss your problems when the goal is to enjoy each other's company...We can decide to be pleasant with our spouse for fifteen minutes a day even if it kills us. What Leah and I actually do during our talk ritual is an emotional check-in...

The third phase of a ritual, after the transition and the enactment, is the exit stage.[5]

What are some ideas for marriage rituals?

- Anniversary kidnapping. Whisk your spouse away to some surprise (you can take turns each year planning). One woman who had been married many years described her kidnapping: "He just sort of scoops me up...and it's really cute. He has a limo pick me up like Cinderella."

- Dick and Kathy explain their marriage ritual: "We were married on the twenty-second of August, and we celebrate each month on the twenty-second. We do something special. It's not necessarily a big thing, but it is every month. This past month, in June, we were married 430 months."

- Take your daily showers together.
- Read aloud to each other at a certain time, perhaps in bed or while one of you does the dishes.
- Kiss when you say hello and goodbye or anytime you exchange the keys to the car.
- Keep an anniversary journal of each year's highlights.
- Go to sleep holding hands. If you go to sleep at different times, meet at the bedside to pray or kiss.
- Take an evening or morning walk and talk.
- Establish an evening activity: dinner each night by candlelight, coffee each night after dinner, a game of chess or cards each night by the fireplace. One couple created a very unique morning ritual: "For twenty minutes every morning, it's just the two of us enjoying a breakfast by candlelight. It's especially romantic during the winter when everything is dark and we talk by candlelight only."

United Marriage Encounter trains couples to dialogue daily by writing on a topic for ten minutes and then talking about it for ten minutes. This laid a fantastic foundation for us and has been instrumental in saving rocky marriages and strengthening solid ones by providing intimate emotional connection.

David and Vera Mace, the founders of the Association for Couples in Marriage Enrichment, also have a daily ritual. David has prepared breakfast and brought it to Vera every morning of their marriage.

Bill and I have a tradition people always comment on. We waited for that first kiss until the day he proposed to me. From that first kiss forward, we always kiss after we say grace at every meal regardless of where we are or who we are with. We've never missed a kiss in more than 25 years! If we even look like we are going to get distracted and forget, one of our kids will scream out, "The kiss! The kiss!"

One of our favorite stories of a marriage ritual comes from a couple who decided that every time they made love, they would put a dollar in the bank and save toward their second honeymoon. Often he'd walk in from work and say, "I got a dollar!" and she'd respond, "I know how to spend it!" Then off they'd go to the bedroom. This ritual happened week after week for years. If they were in a boring business meeting, all she had to do to end the meeting was to slide a dollar bill across the table—business meeting over! Year after year they traded dollar bills back and forth, enjoying satisfying sexual intimacy and adding money to their bank account. For their fiftieth wedding anniversary, they went for several weeks to Hawaii, stayed in all the best places, ate at the nicest restaurants, and enjoyed the most exciting adventures and activities. Their daughter picked them up at LAX, and she said, "At baggage claim Daddy pulled out his wallet, took out a dollar, and said to Mama, 'Want to start saving for Cancún?'"

Rituals are like a great investment. If you do something romantic every day, all those expressions of love are banked away for a rainy day. If things get tough, you have accumulated a wealth in the love bank—and it has accumulated interest!

Get a Mentor

Life is much easier when you have some help from those who are further along the trail. Their wisdom and insight will prove to be invaluable in your own journey together. Mentoring is becoming even more important as the majority of the population today comes from homes that experienced divorce. You may have never lived with both a mother and a father. How are you supposed to know what an intact family looks like? Who is going to model for you how to work through conflict if your own parents decided to abandon their marriage?

Look for a couple who has the love that you'd like to have. Look around and see who holds hands, who acts kind to one another, who opens the door, who prays for one another or for other couples.

Look for a couple who has done what you want to do. Some careers have unique marital pressures: physicians (especially ob-gyn!), politicians, ministry and clergy couples, CEOs and entrepreneurs, and media or military personnel. Look for a couple who have not only survived in your particular fishbowl but thrived and found a life that has served them and their families well.

Look for a couple who lives in your world. They will be stronger mentors if they live in your neighborhood, are a part of your work world, or attend your church. You will be able to see them in a variety of circumstances, and they will be there to answer those day-to-day issues and questions that may crop up. A great way to discover a marriage mentor is to join a marriage enrichment class offered by your church or by organizations like United Marriage Encounter or Marriage Savers. (See www.smartmarriages.com for many options.) By attending a class or conference with a group, you will meet couples who are interested in having a strong marriage, and some of those couples may have some wisdom to share.

Look for a couple who shares something in common with you. We have three sons, and we have enjoyed having mentors who raised all boys. We have benefited from mentors who are clergy couples and ones who are writers and speakers. We have enjoyed attending sporting events with sports-minded mentors, exercising with them, or even vacationing with them.

Look for a couple who is willing. They don't have to be perfect—no couple is! They don't even necessarily need to be trained marriage mentors or professional marriage educators. They just need to have a strong, stable relationship themselves.

Make a list of two to five couples who might be willing to mentor you. Decide which couple might be the best fit and invite them to dinner. See how the dinner goes. Ask them questions about how they met, what advice they would give to newlyweds, and the like. If this dinner goes well, make a follow-up appointment for coffee or dinner. Ask them if they would be willing to spend some time with you. You might suggest they lead you and some friends through a marriage enrichment book if they enjoy teaching. You might ask if they would just be willing to meet for a meal on occasion or be available for questions as they arise. Be sensitive about the amount of time they might have available for you. Decide when you will get together next, and make sure to thank them for their willingness.

Baby Makes Three

The decision to become parents creates a major transition for couples. For some, it involves the strain of adding a 24/7 project to the relationship. For many other couples it involves the stress of infertility. Millions of decisions can follow birth or adoption of a child. Toddlers and preschoolers need a safe environment, freedom to learn, and a small social circle. Selma Fraiberg, while a professor at the University of Michigan, discovered that children under three fared best when cared for by their mother. Those three to six could sustain absence from mother for half a day but did less well with an absence of ten to twelve hours.[6] A couple must ask themselves, "How can we best see that these needs are met?"

Who will care for the kids? A variety of options are available: Dad could work and Mom could stay home full-time, or Mom could work from home full- or part-time (she may or may not need help at home then). Dad could stay home while Mom works, or Mom and Dad could work opposite shifts so a parent is always caring for the child (but you might not see much of each other). You could hire an in-home nanny or au pair or try daycare (choosing from small in-home or larger daycare facilities). A relative may be able to care for the children. These options all have positives and negatives.

No one can love a child like a parent. A couple should list the pros and cons of all the available options. Wise couples will actually do this in the dating stage of their relationship. Parenting values are usually held tightly. Similarly, couples should discuss the number of children they desire and what kind of environment they want to raise them in—in a homeschool, on a farm, in private or public education, near cultural hubs, and so on.

Couples want to do the right thing for their children. A young mother has survived the additional stress of pregnancy and is dealing with its effect on her body and emotions. Our obstetrician offered a great book to all expectant couples: *What to Expect When You're Expecting.* That doctor probably saved a few marriages with that information!

After the baby comes, both parents face some major adjustments. The biggest is adjusting to no sleep and being on call 24/7!

I (Bill) had a huge adjustment when our first son was born. I had never babysat before, and we had no extended family in the area, so I hadn't been around babies. Brock required an emergency C-section, and he was born a dark blue because he had been in fetal distress. When he finally took a breath and his body changed from blue to pink, the doctor tucked him into my arm, and he fit better than any football I'd carried! He was born on New Year's Eve, so on New Year's Day we had our first male bonding experience and watched football in the hospital room all day!

But when we got Brock home, I soon found I was struggling with my emotions. When he cried, Pam ran right to him to fix his every need. When I had a need and expressed it, Pam would say, "Step up, Dad!" I felt as if I was competing for her attention. I soon realized that women have an amazing ability to add people to their lives. I was afraid the love in Pam's heart was going to be divided between the two of us. Nobody told me ahead of time that it was going to grow exponentially with every new person added to the family.

The learning curve and adjustment are gigantic at this early stage, and a wise couple will take extra time to talk and be together as they adjust to their new roles and responsibilities.

But This Isn't What I Signed Up For!

This is a woman's midlife evaluation—and if not handled well it can become a crisis. All women go through this developmental stage. For some it is a process of blooming. For others who are unprepared, it may feel like a personal crisis. Usually between the ages of 28 and 38, a woman will say, "I love my husband and my children, but is this all there is to life—dishes, laundry, responsibility?" Or she might say, "I have been focusing on a career, and now I hear my biological clock ticking." She is asking the big questions of life: *Why am I here? What is my purpose? What is my passion?*

This is when a woman is most likely to have an affair. She has questions deep in her heart, and her husband is often very busy. He may be very focused on work and miss his wife's emotional clues. Some women look for someone else to listen to their heart. Often that someone is a man from work, church, the neighborhood, or a computer chatroom. She never intended to get into an affair, but as her emotional needs began being met not by her husband but by her new friend, the affair happened.

Many women say, "An affair? Yeah, right! How is a woman going to add responsibility for one more person to her life!"

Unfortunately, too many do.

In *The 10 Best Decisions a Woman Can Make* (Harvest House Publishers), I (Pam) share a few decisions that will help a woman safeguard her marriage:

Decide you will communicate with your spouse. He may be very busy trying to build his career and be a good provider for the family, but you can grab him by the lapels as he runs by and say, "I love us too much to let life pull us apart. Can I have some time with you each week?"

Decide you will take your questions to safe circles. Get a mentor, join a small group Bible study, or pay for counseling. Set up boundaries around your marriage and promise yourself you will not share your time or your heart with any male but your spouse.

Decide to develop yourself. Don't become a martyr and whine that you never have time for yourself. Instead, look for ways to nurture your interests, talents, and gifts in ways that fit with the rest of your priorities. Many women bail on their family in an all-or-nothing mentality. Instead, while your kids are in school, finish your education. While your husband relaxes with the guys on the softball field, go to an exercise or art class.

Decide to keep your eyes off yourself. In this stage of life, women can get ingrown eyeballs. I have heard some pretty outrageous statements from midlife women, such as "Can you believe it? My husband works all the time. He never has time for me and the kids." Be reasonable. The world can't come to a screeching halt just because you are in this transition. Your family will still have needs, your spouse will still have a job, your church and community will still value your involvement. I have found that as we face life realistically, God uses real life to answer some of the questions of our heart.

Boy, Life Is Pricey!

While a woman is in midlife evaluation, her man is usually in superman mode, trying to provide for the family. He has come to grips with how expensive his life is going to be and realizes he needs to step up to the plate and not just have a job. He must develop a career that will keep up with the rising demands of the ones he loves most in life.

This realization hit Bill when we moved from the central valley of California to expensive Southern California and Bill took a pay cut to become the senior pastor of a small but soon-to-be-growing church. After spending a discouraging day with a Realtor, we had no hopes of qualifying for a home in a market where houses were increasing in value by $10,000 a month!

One evening, we went to a friend's for dinner. Our two-year-old, Zachery, said, "I'm hungry."

We gave him two hot dogs and a plate of beans.

Again he said, "I'm hungry," and we gave him a hamburger.

Still again we heard, "I'm hungry," so we gave him more beans and dessert.

A crowd gathered around Zach, watching him eat. They nicknamed him Baby Hoover because he was vacuuming up food! Then it hit Bill. *When my sons all get to high school and are all athletes, my food bill will be the same as one of these outrageous Southern California mortgages!* Bill went into warp-speed work mode, trying to create a career that would keep pace with the boys' appetites. We have since passed that season, and he was absolutely right! When our oldest son left for college, our food bill was cut in half!

When a man's family begins to grow, he can experience feelings of fight or flight. He either decides to stay in the marriage and fight to provide for his wife and family, or he says, "This is too hard. I don't feel like being married anymore."

A man is more likely to make the right choice and stay with his family when he has support:

- His wife and children say "thank you" and appreciate his hard work.

- He has a male mentor who can say, "Yes, this is hard, but you can do it!" In healthy families, older men in the extended family fulfill this role. A man who has none of these living nearby can join a men's Bible study and look for a male mentor who loves God and his family.

- He makes time to listen to his wife and play with the kids.

- He pursues tools to build a healthy life, such as attending marriage conferences, buying DVDs, CDs, and books by marriage leaders, joining a Bible study or marriage enrichment group, or paying for counseling by a member of the clergy or a marriage and family counselor. (In the back of this book you'll find the address to our website, where you can find lists of marriage enrichment groups, educators, and suggestions for finding a Christian counselor in your area.)

Marriages break up at this time more often than at any other. In 2002, the median age for men at their first divorce was 30.5. At their second divorce it was 39.3. For women, the median age was 29 and 37 respectively. The median duration of a first marriage that ended in divorce was a little under eight years.[7] People between the ages of 25 and 39 make up 60 percent of all divorces.[8]

Berserk

On the chart at the end of the chapter you will see this stage marked "Families with teenagers," but it is much more. It is when life hits critical mass, and everything seems to pile up at once! Dad is in midlife evaluation, Mom is in menopause or perimenopause, and teens are flooded with hormones. You are paying for college, weddings, medical bills, and past mistakes. You are facing new health challenges in yourselves and in your aging parents. Many families experience incredible stress during this stage as they are forced to deal with unexpected pregnancy and child-care issues or they are wrestling with the juvenile justice system. Yikes! That's why we call this "berserk."

The word *berserk* comes from ancient Norse warriors, who were legendary for working themselves into a frenzy before a battle and fighting with reckless savagery and insane fury. The warriors would frantically fight, regardless of their wounds. The word can sometimes mean "crazed," and that's how life feels at times during this season—just a little insane! The pace of life alone can be overwhelming. Both your careers and volunteer reputations are at their peak.

Mom might seem like she is going berserk because she is entering menopause and feeling lousy—emotionally, physically, or both. In our book *Why Men and Women Act the Way They Do,* we provide four pages of symptoms women might deal with as their hormonal balance changes. Symptoms range from night sweats and hot flashes to much more serious mental issues like depression, anxiety, or suicidal thoughts. Teens might be going berserk because they are trying to figure out who they are while adjusting to their own raging hormonal changes. Dad might be going berserk because he is in the middle of a major life evaluation. He is asking questions such as these:

- Do I want to continue in this career?
- Have my sacrifices been worth it?

- I feel so mortal—how can I feel young again?
- Why do I feel so lost? (Unresolved emotional baggage from his youth may crop back up.)
- I have spent so much time at work—why do I feel like a stranger in my own home?
- I want deep, emotionally connected relationships. Who will listen to my heart?

In his book *Men in Midlife Crisis*, Jim Conway describes feeling like a vending machine because everyone wanted something from him. One day I noted some of the things people wanted from Bill, including his car keys, counsel, money, wisdom, connections, time, talent, resources, prayers, muscles, and expertise. He gave and gave and gave until one day, he gave out. He was faced with a health issue that impacted his career choices.

I (Bill) was diagnosed with high blood pressure, which runs in my family. My grandfather had a stroke when my dad was 17 years old. My dad had a stroke when I was 18! Until I was 43, I had no signs of high blood pressure in my life. Suddenly, it shot up to 150/100, and my world was rocked. I had eaten well and exercised regularly so that I would avoid this trend in my family, but my routine was no longer working. I couldn't keep up the pace I had built my life on for the past two decades.

I was deeply disappointed. Pam was scared. I wrestled with deep feelings of failure for the next year. I felt weak and vulnerable. I found I didn't know how to work without being intensely focused. I had to spend more time thinking about me and my health than I ever had. I felt selfish. For the first time in my adult life, I didn't know how to be me.

I praise God, however, because with some schedule adjustments, good health advice, a severe reduction of sodium intake, exercise, and dietary supplements, I was able to refocus my life and regain my health. The road has not been easy, though. The transition has been huge for me, Pam, our family, and many others in our church and community. I feel as if I'm living half a life compared to all the exciting things I used to do. I know I need to finish this transition, but I sometimes wonder if life will ever feel normal.

Before You Walk Away

Anyone can easily get overwhelmed and want to just walk away. But walking away doesn't help because wherever you go, you take yourself with you. You face the same struggles, same victories, and same issues. Walking away when you still have a chance to rebuild your life together only complicates your life with lawyer fees, extra bills, and part-time parenting. Consider the following coping skills for hanging tough when life pushes you to your limits:

Find a focus. Find a reason to make life worth the effort. You have built a life together. Splitting up might wipe you out financially. Hang in there for the kids. Studies show that kids who have divorced parents are more likely to use drugs, have premarital sex, and get lower grades. Don't make your kids pay the price just because you are unwilling to go the distance. Hang in there to please God. Focus on something bigger than you and more noble than just your personal happiness.

Find emotional support. Decide not to seek outside opposite-sex relationships to make yourself feel better. Instead, find a friend of the same gender who has made it through. Don't look to your divorced or single friends for support—they can contribute to the decay of a marriage. Instead, attend a men's, women's, or couples' Bible study. Start a prayer group for couples or ladies. Ladies, start a Wives in Prayer group or a Seasoned Sisters group.[9] It's hard to stay mad at someone you pray for!

Find an oasis. Start exercising together or take up an exciting new activity, as Jim Conway did. He and his wife, Sally, wrote *When a Mate Wants Out: Secrets for Saving a Marriage.* Jim took up sailing. Usually he would sail alone to think about life, but at times the family would join him. You both have worked hard, and this life stage is strenuous. Find something that replenishes you. Bill and I have taken up tennis dates. Other friends ballroom dance, and others bought a cabin hideaway. Whatever your preference, do something constructive to build new happy memories in the midst of what might feel like chaos.

Best of Days

Our friends Dave and Claudia Arp, authors of *The Second Half of Marriage*, say, "The rest can be the best!" If you hang in there, you will enjoy a payoff! Second honeymoons really do happen! The kids get married, leave home (you hope!), and stay gone (you hope)! Recently, more grandparents have been raising grandkids. Five to six percent of grandkids live with grandparents for a portion of their lives, but most couples get some significant time together after 50 years of age.[10] Most grandparents say that grandkids are a big part of the payoff! This is your turn to buy all those noisy, annoying toys and send them home with your kids when the grandkids come to visit. And you get to give the grandkids candy and soda before you send them home while you imagine the fun your kids will have with them!

Look for an adventure you can do together. Make a list of all the things you want to make sure you do before you die, and start checking off the list! Use this time to invest in truly meaningful work and volunteer work like building homes for Habitat for Humanity or being substitute missionary school parents. Travel in your RV and donate time to camps and conference centers. Start a second business or volunteer for political or social causes.

We know a couple who awkwardly discovered one of the greatest adventures of their lives. She created a successful home-based gardening business that required quite a bit of her time. When he retired, he followed her around the garden, hoping to get her attention. She grew frustrated with his consistent interruptions, so one day she asked him to take pictures of the garden for a presentation she had to make. They found out he was a great photographer, and now magazines send them around the world. She writes articles, and he takes pictures of gardens.

This is also the perfect time of life to mentor marriages. Mike

McManus of Marriage Savers writes about a reform his church made for couples getting married:

> The major reform our church pioneered was to train older, solidly married couples to give the inventory and mentor those preparing for marriage. Instead of having a pastor go over the results in an hour or two, mentor couples, whose kids are grown, can spend four or five evenings, reviewing every item. This is a lavish investment of time, giving young couples what may be their first exposure to a vibrant, joyful marriage...Of 302 couples who registered for our course between 1992 and 2000, 21 dropped out and 34 couples broke their engagement before there was a wedding, according to Catherine Latimer, who studied our church's results. But she reports there have been only five divorces and two separations of those who married. "That means there is only a 2.5 percent failure rate over a course of almost 10 years. Compare that to the 50 percent divorce rate," Miss Latimer writes. "This is not just marriage preparation. This is marriage insurance."[11]

Before You Say Goodbye

Watching the one you have loved for a lifetime struggle with health issues or pass from this earth is never easy. But it can be powerful to watch this kind of lasting love in action. While visiting my (Pam's) grandparents for their sixtieth wedding anniversary, I asked them, "Grandma and Grandpa, you know Bill and I speak on marriage. What is your secret to a lasting, happy marriage?" Grandmother looked at Grandpa, smiled, and laughed, "Honey, pure grit and determination!"

My grandmother struggled with her health and was on oxygen. One night she was having difficulty breathing, so she woke Grandpa up. "Gerald, do you think you can hold me? I'm having a hard time breathing." He wrapped his arms around the bride of his youth, the woman he had loved since she was 14. He gently rocked her back and forth until he rocked her right into the arms of Jesus. That is the way I want to go out of this world—wrapped in the arms of the one I love!

The Secret

During these tough transitions, husbands and wives can easily blame each other for the stress in the relationship. One day, during a particularly strenuous time of life, I was complaining to Bill.

"Honey, why is life so stressful? What are you doing? What am I doing wrong?" Bill just smiled at me as I reeled off a list of stress factors, including the age of our kids and the demands of our careers.

"Angel, it's not you. It's not me. It's just life." And as I considered the items I had just listed, I realized he was completely correct. Some seasons of marriage and some stages of life are just more strenuous and more stressful, even if everybody is doing everything correctly. Every person has to go through transitions, and nothing is gained in the blame game. Things only get worse if you attack your teammate in life. Today, wrap your arms around each other, look one another in the eyes and say, "It's not you. It's not me. It's just life!"

Look at the chart on the next page. Where are you now? What transitions have you already tackled? What transitions are ahead? Remember, this is a chart of the average couple. Your chart may look very different, particularly if you married later in life or this is not your first marriage. Talk through the transitions and issues ahead and what you can do now to better prepare for them. Ask a couple you respect who has successfully navigated transitions ahead of you, "What tough time do you remember? What did you do right during that time that you believe helped you become stronger as a couple or more in love as a result?"

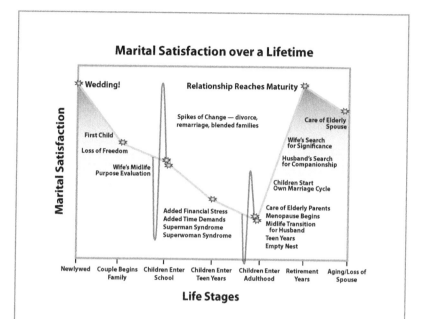

Marital Satisfaction over a Lifetime

(y-axis) Marital Satisfaction

(x-axis) Life Stages

Newlywed | Couple Begins Family | Children Enter School | Children Enter Teen Years | Children Enter Adulthood | Retirement Years | Aging/Loss of Spouse

Labels within chart:
- Wedding!
- Relationship Reaches Maturity
- First Child
- Loss of Freedom
- Wife's Midlife Purpose Evaluation
- Spikes of Change — divorce, remarriage, blended families
- Care of Elderly Spouse
- Wife's Search for Significance
- Husband's Search for Companionship
- Children Start Own Marriage Cycle
- Added Financial Stress
- Added Time Demands
- Superman Syndrome
- Superwoman Syndrome
- Care of Elderly Parents
- Menopause Begins
- Midlife Transition for Husband
- Teen Years
- Empty Nest

This chart is based on our experience working with couples. It tracks the general satisfaction of the "average" marriage. The spikes of change reveal that many factors can impact your own satisfaction. For example, divorce, remarriage, and a blended family can bring trauma as well as positive emotions and many adjustments. Your own personal chart might also be impacted by having children out of wedlock, infertility, or delaying having children. Some transitions can happen almost all at once. For example, having a baby at forty might mean toddlers, hot flashes, and dealing with a midlife husband all at once. Blending a family might mean all that plus dealing with teens and the stress of paying for college, weddings, and graduations. But if you learn about typical transitions, your overall satisfaction will increase because you will be better prepared for life and love.[12]

Decide to Leave
a Legacy of Love

*Love does not delight in evil
but rejoices with the truth.*

*Marriage is when a man and woman become as one.
The trouble starts when they try to decide which one.*

For our twenty-fifth wedding anniversary, we gave each of our sons a ring with a family crest Bill and I designed. We wanted the boys to have an heirloom that they could pass down from generation to generation and that would symbolize the values the Farrel family stands for. The crest looks like this:*

The three *L*s down the center stand for *Learner, Leader,* and *Lover of God.* Each year from the time our oldest was four, we have had a

---

* Artwork by Lucas Graciano.

Learner and Leader Day. That's the day we negotiate privileges and responsibilities, select one leadership trait to focus on for each son that year, and give a gift that applauds the uniqueness we see God building in each of their lives. (More details on how to do a Learner and Leader Day and other parenting tips are in our book *The 10 Best Decisions Every Parent Can Make* [Harvest House Publishers].)

We want our sons to be known for these traits:

Learners. We want them to compete in life and be willing to do the hard work to learn and become excellent.

Leaders. We want them to use their own unique leadership styles to influence others.

Lovers of God. We want them to own their *own* faith.

The cross with the star rising from it represents that we want them to seek God's vision for their life. We want God's heart to be the source of all their hopes, dreams, and desires.

The two interlocking hearts represent integrity and commitment. When a Farrel says something, we want it to be truth, and we want to be known as a family who keeps all of our commitments—especially the marriage covenant.

Inside the ring is inscribed the verse and phrase we used as the motto by which we raised our sons: "No good thing does God withhold from those who walk uprightly" (see Psalm 84:11 NASB). Our job is to walk uprightly; God's job is to decide what good things will come as a reward. In other words, those who honor God, God honors. Somehow, some way, God places His hand of anointing and strength on those who have a pure heart and walk. When the boys feel as if the narrow road is too confining, we want them to remember the walk is worth the effort.

Now you try. What do you want your family to be known for? What are your core values, those three or four traits you want your children, grandchildren, and great-grandchildren to possess? As you answer these questions, draw a symbol in the crest below that explains your value system.

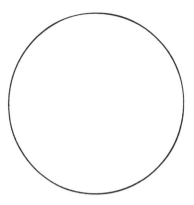

Use your crest and the questions at the end of the chapter to write your own marriage mission statement. As a sample, here's our mission statement, which we created years ago:

> We, Bill and Pam Farrel, have a desire to fulfill the Great Commission, using our skills in professional ministry, with a focus of using the communication gifts God has given us. We are committed to personal discipleship as a lifestyle. We want our home to be an oasis where those who enter can see Christ at work in our marriage and family and where they can find hope. We are committed to fun and friendships. We value people more than things. We prefer memories over material goods. We are committed to raise our children in such a way as they have the opportunity to know the benefits of personally knowing Jesus and walking with Him. We are committed to helping them discover their talents and equipping them to help fulfill the Great Commission and to have fun and a fulfilling life while doing so.

Decide to leave a legacy of love. Decide your love will lay a strong foundation for future generations to build on. Decide to be the example of long-lasting love. We have discovered it is easier to pass on love's principles when we have clearly thought them out and communicated them. We encourage you to set aside a date night this week and create three items:

A family mission. Use the mission statement above as an example. Determine the values, beliefs, and traditions you hold dear and write down a marriage mission statement you can post.

A family motto. A mission statement is often too long to memorize, but if you shorten it to a motto, your children and grandchildren can assimilate it easily. For Christmas the year of our twenty-seventh anniversary, I told my sons, "I don't want gifts, just words that will make me cry." Bill had each son send a letter, which he placed over a photo of that son "in action." Each one of those tributes contained the words, "Those who honor God, God honors." The baton had been securely passed, our sons had the family motto inscribed on their hearts.

A family moniker. Our sons went to private schools for a portion of their education. These schools all had emblems that pictured the core values of the school. We also work with military couples to help them build marriages and each branch of the Armed Forces has an emblem that captures the heart and soul of that branch of service. In the same way, a family crest can be the symbol of your family's strengths and core values. Take the time to design this. If your children are older, you might want to include them in the brainstorming session and then assign the most artistic child to create the color version you can then post in your home.

Epic Love

Why commit to all this work? Because a marriage with a clear, well-defined purpose gives you a reason bigger than yourself and your personal happiness to stay together and work to build a love that lasts. I (Pam) want a love that changes the world for the better.

My favorite story of a love like this comes from Reverend Walter and Matilda Duff. As a young man in Ireland, Walter led hundreds to Christ. Later, he felt God was calling him to be a missionary to China. His father tried to talk him out of it, even offering to fund two others to go to China in his place! When his family saw he was serious about entering the ministry, his father informed Walter that he would have no part in the family's fortune. He would be completely on his own. Determined to follow God's will, he entered seminary and married. Matilda obviously didn't marry for money! The Duffs lived on faith and love and probably a good measure of soup and bread!

Soon Walter felt called to pastor in America. He came to the States ahead of his immigrating Irish family. Walter and Matilda had four children: Helen, Evangeline, Walter, and Olive. He booked passage for his family on the safest vessel of the day. Matilda missed her husband desperately, so she changed the travel arrangements, and the family set sail two weeks earlier. The children couldn't help but notice the providence of God as they heard the newspaper boy shout out about the boat that they were originally supposed to be on: "*Extra! Extra! Titanic Sinks!*"

Following in the Footsteps

That amazing love birthed more amazing love. The Duff teens noticed that many community churches lacked leadership and their buildings were in need of repair. Helen describes one church that stood out in her memory as "very dilapidated...The windows were all broken out, the door hanging open, and strange to say, the big pulpit Bible was lying open on the pulpit, its pages flipping back and forth in the wind."[1] Soon the Duff sisters found themselves traveling through rural America, singing and planting Sunday schools, vacation Bible schools, and other creative works. Their efforts often resulted in the formation of a new congregation or the strengthening of a small or weary congregation that longed for the quality teaching and leadership the girls provided.

The girls soon married. Helen founded Christian Women's Clubs, which underwrote the placement of pastors in rural communities. Later, because this work grew, a new organization was formed to provide leadership for rural churches: Village Missions. Helen's brother, Pastor Walter Duff, eventually took the helm of Village Missions. This movement now serves in more than 250 locations in America and more than 30 in Canada.

The Christian Women's Clubs expanded their own ministry and formed Professional Couples' Clubs. Bible coffees for follow-up and discipleship naturally followed. And all these outreach ministries needed booklets and other written information, so a publishing company sprang up to meet the need. Stonecroft Ministries is now over 1800 groups strong, has published an assortment of resources distributed worldwide, has 1600 local representatives, and has 1400 people in leadership. Stonecroft Ministries exists in all 50 states and 61 foreign countries.

While Helen and Walter were working with Stonecroft Ministries and Village Missions, their sister and brother-in-law, Evangeline and Archie McNeill, both had a strong impression that God was leading them into conference ministry. They found the property which would eventually become Cannon Beach Christian Conference Center. Archie McNeill's original vision was for Cannon Beach to provide a "vacation with a purpose."[2] Now, Cannon Beach Christian Conference Center hosts more than 150 conference groups a year with a total attendance between 400,000 and 500,000. It also hosts Ecola Bible School, which was started by Evangeline McNeill's nephew, David Duff. Evangeline's son, Haldane, became a pastor and served on the board of Cannon Beach for many years, while Evangeline's daughter led the conference center for many years.

Cannon Beach Christian Conference Center, Stonecroft Ministries, Village Church Missions, Ecola Bible School—are you grasping how *one couple's love* impacted the world for good in such an amazing way? It all started because Matilda was heartsick and missed her precious husband! Oh, for more couples with an epic love story like this.

Your Love, a Light

You can decide how your love will shine. Every family has a personality or unique gift that can leave a positive imprint in the world. Have you noticed that often skills related to music, teaching, health care, ministry, leadership, or politics run in families? Several sets of presidents were related, most recently George H.W. Bush and George W. Bush, and Jeb Bush was governor of Florida. The Kennedy dynasty served for years as America's "royal" family. Consider the Graham family. Nearly all of Billy and Ruth Graham's children serve in full-time international leadership in ministry as communicators and leaders of organizations.

To get ideas about your family's future, look back at your own lives for spiritual markers. You have had some unique experiences that have prepared your family for the road ahead. You might have had a unique upbringing, or you might have a unique pain.

Your family may have generations of great traditions and strong leaders. Pastor John MacArthur and Dr. David Jeremiah are both products of generations of pastors. Our friends the Storms have a picture of their extended family. It took Nancy almost ten minutes to name each person and his or her professional ministry calling. Her in-laws created a family atmosphere that fostered a heart for ministry service. When we were in Germany, speaking to American troops and their spouses, we were struck by the number of those in the military who grew up in the military.

Looking back into your family tree can give glimpses of what might come naturally to you. For example, family values come easy for me (Pam) because I have a legacy of family sticking together through thick and thin. Bill's parents were from the South, and mine grew up on ranches, so the values of country living are in our hearts. People always come before programs or procedure. Friendship, loyalty, and an open-door policy thrive in our home. We always have extra kids spending the night and often have people living with us or eating with us. All through our kids' high school experience we had a 12-passenger van (affectionately nicknamed Wheezy for the way it sputtered to start). The van wasn't for us but for all the youth groups, sports teams, and Christian rock bands who needed to use it.

We also have sports genes. Both Bill and I were athletes growing up. My (Pam) dad was a competitive cowboy, as was his father. Bill's dad was a fighter pilot. Being competitive is a trait that comes easily for all three of our sons. They have the basic skills for athletics, and our family environment encourages their development. Having our oldest son start a Fellowship of Christian Athletes chapter on his high school campus and having both of us serve on the FCA board was a no-brainer and our hearts' desire. Our sons started a sports camp called "Future Champs Camp" to help young boys become men by using sports as the platform for hands-on learning.

Every family has a style of operation. As a family, you rely on this style, revert to this style under stress, and enjoy life when this style is in full operation. Listed below are a number of family styles. See if you can identify your family in one of these styles and begin to set goals for your family based on your style.

Focused Families: What Is Your Style?

The leadership family. These families are characterized by action, they are up-front, they are in charge, and they influence their communities. They are dependable when leading events and organizations in church, school, and in the community. God uses these families to build more leaders generation after generation. Their greatest contribution is their decision-making ability. Their key motivation is influence. The downside of this family style is that if they are not leading, they can become harsh and critical. Leaders were meant to lead.

The missionary family. Love in these families is as big as the world. They take the initiative to reach out, share their faith, gain a world focus, or travel the world. They enjoy different cultures and are willing to invest time and money to be educated, learn languages, and build relationships with those of other cultures. God uses these families to build bridges and break down barriers. Their greatest contribution is their ability to open doors of opportunity to impact other cultures. They are motivated when they see change. The downside of this family is that if they aren't reaching out, they shrink back and become timid as if they have lost hope.

The hospitable family. Love is expressed with an open-door, open-arms, open-home policy. These families live in homes that are organized and friendly, and their life is safe and predictable, so others feel comfortable around them. They create a stable environment with routines, preparation, and attention to detail. They enjoy serving others, so God uses these homes to raise children with servant attitudes. Their greatest contribution is that their homes are havens of hope and help to those who enter. They are motivated by relationships. If these families turn inward instead of outward, they become self-absorbed, building castles for self-indulgence instead of caring centers of hope.

The generous family. Love is expressed by giving. These families are good networkers, ambitious, and focused on others, and they love sharing their time, talent, and treasures. They rejoice with those who rejoice and weep with those who weep. They enjoy helping others succeed. They have a family culture of support. Their greatest contribution is their commitment to strengthen and be a resource for other people's ministries. Several of our friends with this family style have family foundations that give away thousands of dollars to worthy causes each year. They are motivated by success and by seeing positive results from their sharing. The downside of these families is that if they do not give, they become restless, flitting from activity to activity without focus, and often their funding becomes untapped or unfocused.

The servant family. Love is expressed by serving in tangible ways. These families are humble, hardworking, unselfish, industrious, and do not want attention for what they do. They are comfortable meeting needs, so their home has a culture of helping out and pitching in. They don't necessarily come up with ideas, but when they see a good one, they jump in wholeheartedly. Their greatest contribution is that God's work is stabilized and secured by these families. They can always be counted on and are motivated by feeling needed. When they don't serve, they can be prone to wander, not knowing where or how to plug in to make a difference.

The encouraging family. Love is expressed by compassion. These families are empathetic, and they want to help people heal (emotionally, physically, or spiritually). They are involved with people, patient, forgiving, and seemingly tireless in their ability to walk next to people.

Their greatest contribution is their ability to prepare people for future service by ensuring recovery and renewal. When these families don't encourage, they can become lethargic.

The teaching family. Love is expressed by the impartation of information. These households are predictable, disciplined, organized, and committed to process. They have a family culture of helping people learn. They are patient, they are researchers, and they always have a way to discover an answer or solution. Their greatest contribution is their ability to prepare people to pass on truth. They are motivated by knowing they are helping maintain a standard of truth. If they don't teach, they can become introspective, turning all their time and energy on themselves rather than on others who need it more.

The expressive family. Love is expressed in artistic, creative, and spontaneous ways in these homes. These families are intense, idealistic, easily excited, and sometimes unconventional. Their greatest contribution is inspiration. They move us through works of art, dance, music, writing, or drama. They are motivated if they can emotionally touch lives. If they don't create or express, they can become erratic and unpredictable.

Which family style(s) most closely resemble(s) your family?

- leadership family
- missionary family
- hospitable family
- generous family
- servant family
- encouraging family
- teaching family
- expressive family

We have observed that some families take and some families give. Families who give usually have kids who excel in school, socially and morally, as they are led by example in traits that form a strong person and a strong society. Create a family that gives. Discover and live out your unique family focus.

You can start a loving legacy. What do you want to remain in the hearts and lives of those who are in the wake of your life and love? Each day we have the opportunity to live out the legacy we want to leave. Here are some ideas to sharpen your focus:

1. List two or three things you enjoy doing as a couple that you think make the world a better place.

2. What does your family enjoy doing, or what is it known for?

3. What is unique about you? What do you do as a married couple and family that few families or couples do?

4. What are the spiritual markers that might point to the future God has for you?

5. What legacy do you want to leave for future generations when you are gone? If you moved from your hometown, what would you want people to miss about your family? How would they complete this sentence: "It's just not the same without you around here. You always..."

6. What are your favorite verses, mottos, and quotes? (Use them in your mission statement.)

7. Write a mission statement.

10

Decide to Connect to the Author of Love

Love always protects, always trusts, always hopes, always perseveres. Love never fails.

May you grow old on one pillow.

—ARMENIAN TOAST

The first fight Bill and I had occurred during our first attempt to study the Bible together. How very strange is that? It is a picture of just how serious Satan is at wreaking havoc on marriages. Maybe you have had a fight on the way to church or deciding whether to go to church.

Consider these statistics:

- The divorce rate for first-time marriages is about 50 percent. However, those who pray together daily have a divorce rate of less than 1 percent!
- Couples who pray together rate their sex life with the highest possible rating.
- Couples who attend a weekly church worship service also give their sex life the highest satisfaction rating.
- Couples whose friends believe in long-term, monogamous marriage tend to have long-term happy marriages. These friends might be found in the local church.

Do you see the pattern? The more spiritual your marriage is, the more likely it is to be successful and sexually satisfying. The more passion you have toward God, the more you'll have available for your marriage.

Do you see why Satan wants to keep you from praying, from reading the Bible, from getting to church? He knows those things will make a change for the better in your relationship.

So if spirituality is the most powerful tool in building a long-term, happy, and sexually satisfying relationship, how does a couple go about building their spiritual life?

Decide to. That's plain and simple. Decide that a spiritual life is just as important as being at the kids' soccer games. It is as valuable as that weekly tee time or tennis match. Decide that time praying with your spouse each day is as vital as your daily shower or daily stop at Starbucks. Decide to check in with the Master Builder, or the Architect of love: God.

Our mentors in ministry are Jim and Sally Conway. In their book *Traits of a Lasting Marriage,* they reveal the secret to long-term, happy marriages. Get your pen out and get ready to write down this earth-shattering discovery: Couples who have long-term, happy marriages *decide* to have long-term, happy marriages. *Duh!* This seems simple, but it's hard to apply in daily life. Decide that today will be the day to spiritually build up your marriage. Then check to see if you have all the tools you need:

- **T** alk to God.
- **O** bey the truth.
- **O** vercome evil.
- **L** ook in the Bible.
- **S** hare with others.

Talk to God

Couples who pray together stay together.

One weekend, Bill and I traveled to a church to speak. While there, one couple seemed to be highly influential. We heard about their love at nearly every home and every leadership circle we were in while in the city. This couple had been married nearly 50 years, and they had a simple habit that had a profound impact not only on their love but on hundreds of other people also. Each morning, this couple had coffee together, just as many other couples do. But over coffee, they discussed what was coming up in each other's day. Then they simply said a sentence or two of blessing over each other as they prayed for one another's requests. When they were done, they kissed and started off on their separate paths with their hearts knit together. They were proficient with the first tool: *Talk to God.*

I (Pam) stayed in a home in Indiana after an all-night flight. The couple so impressed me that years later I still remember them fondly. He was the most positive, affirming man I had ever met (other than Bill). I arrived at 6:30 a.m. and just had time to take a shower and rush off to speak at their church. She was so hospitable and he was so positive that I longed to sit leisurely over their breakfast table and learn more about how other couples could have this same atmosphere in their home. He was complimentary of his wife, of me, and of the director of women's ministry, who was driving me. His wife was so gracious, helpful, and hospitable. Both had such amazing servant's attitudes and such a positive outlook on life that on the way to the church I commented to the director of women's ministry, "Wow! They're amazing! Are they always that positive and affirming and kind to each other?"

She smiled, "Always! And they are that way to everyone in their world! I've known them all my life."

"I feel cheated then! I wish I would have known them all my life! I wish I could clone or bottle what they have in their marriage. Our world would be a much better place, and I know of a whole lot of marriages that would be saved."

I remember the way the husband prayed for each person at the breakfast table. It wasn't just a prayer. It was more of a blessing, listing positive traits in each of us as he asked God to bless and anoint our day. I felt so empowered even though I was functioning on no sleep! What I gained that day was far better refreshment than a few hours of shut-eye would have given me! I gained insight that enhanced my own love and that I have passed on to others.

Why pray? We have seen amazing statistics showing that prayer works like glue in a marriage, and we have personally witnessed the power of prayer. Prayer is like a window to the heart of your spouse. We are rarely phony in prayer. We rarely stay angry at someone when we listen in on their conversations with God. People reveal more about themselves in prayer than any other form of communication. They drop the excuses and masks. They open up and are vulnerable before God. Because prayer is intimacy with God, a natural by-product of praying together is intimacy with each other.

Even one person praying can impact a marriage. We were once on a television show with a country singing artist. He told of how his wife expressed her love to him when he was living far from God. She would wrap herself next to him in bed, stroke his chest or his back, and pray blessings aloud over him. At first, he said he was irritated because she knew he didn't really believe in God. But then he began to see God answering some of the requests. Before long, he began to ask his wife to pray over certain areas of his life and responsibilities. He began to rely on her and those nightly prayers so much that if he was on the road, he'd call home for them. Even if she was sleepy and dozing off, he'd wake her up to pray over him! Finally, love broke through, and on one of those nights in bed, he prayed and asked Christ into his life. Now they pray together, asking God's blessings over one another each night.

Louis Evans, a former pastor of the Hollywood Presbyterian Church, said he never knew a couple who divorced after praying together, on their knees, every day for a week. Dr. Paul Tournier wrote that "when each of the marriage partners seeks quietly before God to see his own faults, recognizes his sin and asks forgiveness of the other, marital problems are no more...They learn to be absolutely honest with each other."[1] Prayer is just being honest with God. Prayer in marriage is being so honest that you allow your spouse to eavesdrop on the conversation. The real you is expressed in prayer.

Bill and I pray several times a day together. As we head out the door, we check in on each other's day and pray with our arms around each other. In the middle of the day, either as we meet for lunch or over the phone, we'll pray for each other. Every night at dinner and again as we fall asleep we say a simple prayer for each other. These prayers often aren't long or particularly spiritual, but they are always honest. Even when we are mad at each other we pray, "God, we aren't doing very well. Help!"

Our favorite and most intimate moments of prayer have been prayers of thanks after we have made love and are still entwined.

How to Pray

God cares more about the attitude of your heart than any formula, rule, or words you might use in prayer. But because prayer can be so intensely personal and emotional, couples often ask how they can pray together.

We like to use this simple acrostic when we pray. Consider the FACTS of prayer:

- *First turn is God's.* We like to read a portion of Scripture and then pause for a moment of silence as we contemplate its meaning and listen for God's Holy Spirit to make some impression on our heart or to our mind.

- *Adoration.* Together we praise God for His character and attributes. Often, we will simply list from *A* to *Z* the qualities we value in God. For example, He is awesome, beautiful, caring, and so on.

- *Confession.* When we pray together, we usually name the areas of sin and the shortcomings we are struggling with. This not only wipes the slate clean with God but also breaks down barriers and walls with each other.

If I (Pam) hear Bill confess he has been struggling with selfishness, fear of failure, or any other issue, I gain compassion and understand why he might have been acting a certain way. Prayer is a window into the heart.

Also, when I hear Bill praying through an area of life, I can be assured that God has his attention. This cuts down nagging. I don't have to remind Bill of anything God's Spirit is already talking to him about!

- *Thanksgiving.* This is appreciating God for what He has already done. It is counting your blessings. One way to get over negative feelings toward your mate is to pray together and thank God for each other. As you hold each other, list as many wonderful positive traits about your spouse as you can think of. This usually makes you realize you had pretty good taste when you picked out the one you love! When you belittle and criticize your spouse, you are really slamming your own ability to make a good decision! Instead, compliment yourself and God by affirming your mate in prayer (and other times too!).

- *Shopping list.* This is when you present to God the requests that are on your heart for yourself, your mate, your family, and your world. Picture God as a benevolent Parent who wants to give you what is best for you. God can see the full picture.

At a conference where we were speaking, we met a woman who walked in on her husband in bed with her best friend. She didn't know what to do, but like most women would, she wanted to either kill him or divorce him. When she prayed, however, she sensed that God wanted her to forgive him.

Then she prayed, *How?* Slowly, day by day, God revealed specific things she could do, say, and think. Unfortunately, he wanted out of the marriage. He said some very hurtful things to her, such as "I hate you. I was never in love with you!"

Her connection to God was so strong that she simply replied with the truth: "I don't receive that. I don't believe that. I loved you when I said, 'I do,' and I believe you loved me then too."

For months he continued to distance himself from her and to say hurtful things. She continued to answer calmly with the truth. She voiced her commitment to their marriage again one night after he had reeled out a list of very hurtful comments. She quietly and confidently answered, "I love you. I choose to love you. I have already proven that nothing will drive you away from my love. I choose to stay with you, and I believe that is the choice you want to make too."

Her husband knelt down, held on to her skirt, put his head into her lap, and sobbed. He told her later that he was so unkind to her because he felt so unworthy of her and her love. He was pushing her away, threatening to leave her before she could leave him. He was afraid he couldn't survive emotionally if she left. Her unconditional love, her commitment to the truth, and her prayers turned their marriage around.

Today, years later, he adores her, and they have more children and a happy, stable life together. Their trials could have destroyed their love, but God turned them into the very nails that held their love together!

Obey the Truth

Kurt and Sherri have been married 25 years. When we asked them what was the happiest day of their lives other than their wedding day, Kurt answered, "The Easter I came to Christ." Sherri went on to explain that Kurt asked Christ into his life on Easter. A few weeks later, on Mother's Day, Sherri made the decision to accept Christ as her Savior. Their son made the same decision a week later, and their daughter two weeks after that. Within just over a month their entire family experienced a radical life transformation.

Kurt and Sherri agreed their marriage was sliding downhill before they came to Christ. They are very different from one another. Kurt is laid-back and calm. Sherri is high-energy and highly motivated. They view money differently. One is a spender, the other a saver. Sherri gets an idea and thinks Kurt should do it. Before he met Christ, Kurt often responded to her ideas with, "Hey, wait a minute. I thought I was in charge here!"

When asked what advice they'd give to newlyweds, Kurt said, "One of the reasons I married Sherri is that she was committed to persevere. And when we first got married, I also knew I had made a commitment. When things got tough, I'd say, 'I made a commitment before God. Breaking the commitment is not an option. The vow was once and for all.' I try to put on God's glasses and look at Sherri the same way God does."

Sherri smiled at her husband with admiration and added that when things get hard for a couple, they should "go back to simplicity. Ask, 'Whom did I fall in love with?' Go back and start dating again." When things get really complicated, Sherri will say, "Let's just go to the movies and hold hands!"

She says, "The battle belongs to the Lord. Sometimes life is a roller coaster, and unless you are both firm in your faith and believe all that God says in His Word, Satan can pull you apart."

Kurt agrees. "Long-term love is 100 percent God's grace. When I am not satisfied with Sherri or one of her behaviors is bothering me, I know God is working in *my* life."

Sherri nods in agreement. "And if I am frustrated, I work out the problem by taking it to God in prayer. As soon as we are both humble and we pray, God sends an answer."

Galatians 5:25 says, "Since we live by the Spirit, let us keep in step with the Spirit." We keep in step with God through obedience, moment by moment. Do whatever He tells you, as soon as He tells you.

Many steps of obedience can actually work like glue to move a couple closer together spiritually. Just last week, Bill and I met a couple married nearly 50 years who were baptized together many years ago. A statement that you are both followers of God can act like superglue for the soul. Fasting can be helpful if you are trying to make a decision and become like-minded, or if one of you is in need. Other disciplines of the faith that can knit souls together include communion, contemplation, meditation at a spiritual retreat center, or simply going for a walk and prayer time.

One of our favorite traditions is to go to Hume Lake Conference Center and hike up to a cross at Inspiration Point to leave our prayer requests in the "little brown chapel." We always go to Hume when we need renewal or wisdom. When we were newlyweds, we often went to the beach. Bill would play his guitar, and we would sing, praise God, and pray together. Worshipping, either with groups or as a couple, is still one of the activities that draw our hearts together as we both focus heavenward.

Overcome Evil

Sometimes you can't find any real issue, any real problem. You just get irritated or dissatisfied with your spouse. If you are in the public eye or are in leadership, the stakes are higher and the attacks on your marriage can be more intense. Years ago, comedian Flip Wilson popularized the line, "The devil made me do it!"

We must not negate our personal responsibility in any way. We are all 100 percent responsible for our actions, attitudes, and words. But Satan has a stake in creating conflict. In 1 Corinthians 14:33, the apostle Paul explains that God is not a God of disorder (NIV) or confusion (NASB). Satan is God's enemy, and his favorite tool is confusion! Satan wants you to misunderstand your spouse's words. He wants you to misinterpret his or her actions toward you. Your love may be intact and healthy, but in his house of mirrors, your perception can be distorted. That's how Satan works. The best way to handle these distortions is to grab hands and pray out loud, *Jesus, Your love is greater than our problem. Your Word says we love because You first loved us. So through Your blood on the cross, we take our stand in You. We command Satan and all of his demons to leave us alone right now! God, Your love is greater!* Overcome evil with good!

The couples who regularly stand up for their marriage and command Satan out of their presence have very strong marriages that nothing seems to be able to rock. They have survived layoffs, prodigals' rebellious years, financial setbacks, personality differences, and anything else that comes their way. They have a confidence that says, "Don't mess with our love!"

We have found that whatever we are writing and teaching on becomes Satan's favorite place to attack. Satan wants to undermine credibility. For example, our first marriage book was titled *Pure Pleasure,* and it was about sexuality. We have a sex life that is frequent, fulfilling, and fun. But as we wrapped that book up and were getting ready to send it in to the publishers, we were at each other's throats! I (Pam) was so concerned, I began researching marital intervention programs and centers and getting cost estimates to see where we could go the day we sent off the manuscript. I brought a list to Bill to lobby him to go. Bill said, "Pam, I love you. You know I would do anything for you. And you love me, right?" I nodded. "Before we spend all this time and money, let's see if we can figure out the issues we are dealing with." Then he listed issue after issue and asked, "Is it this?" My answer was always no.

"Honey," I asked, "why is it that we seem to have no real issue but I am so mad at you?"

"I think Satan wants us to be mad at each other," he replied. "We are role models of healthy sexuality, and that makes Satan mad."

I said, "Then I am about to make Satan really mad!" I grabbed Bill's hand and led him into our bedroom. We prayed and enjoyed each other, thumbing our noses at Satan with our love.

Look in the Bible

Often, God's Word provides a backdrop for our thinking. It provides perspective. Our friends Randy and Debe have been married 30 years. Debe explains one view of how God's Word provides perspective:

> "I don't know how we'll ever fill up this big house!" I still remember those words as if they were yesterday. Thirty

years ago, as a young newlywed, that was my perspective as I stood in the middle of our new home. How my perspective changed 20 years and four children later! I stood in the same house and said, "This little house just isn't big enough for all of us!"

Our daughter was coming home after a year away at college, and I felt it was important for her to have her own room. Then the thought hit me...the garage! We could convert part of the garage into a room for her. All that occupied our garage was Randy's boat, tools, and fishing gear (my perspective). When I first suggested this idea to him, his first reaction was that he needed a room to protect his boat (his perspective). To that I replied, "What is more important to you: to protect your boat or your daughter?" (No guilt intended, of course.) At that, his perspective quickly shifted. He looked a little sheepish and then set out for Home Depot to get the materials for our new remodel.

When your thinking is guided by God's Word, you will naturally look for the win-win in love.

Being in God's Word daily impacts the way you think and feel. On our wedding gifts to each other, we inscribed the words from 1 John 4:19 (GNT), "We love because God first loved us." The same book of the Bible teaches us that God is love, so one way to see immediate results in your marriage is to spend time with the Author of love each day in His Word. You will begin to reflect love to those around you. You will make decisions to love. Debe goes on to share a day when love reigned in her home:

> Some couples dream of having a little house with a white picket fence, two cats in the yard, and a porch with a little swing. Although all that sounds nice, all I ever really wanted was to have a fireplace. When my husband and I searched for our first home, this was a definite priority. We finally narrowed it down to the house that we have been

living in for the past 30 years. The first thing I noticed when we drove up to the house was that it was without a chimney...no fireplace. I didn't have to say a word. As we stood in the middle of the living room, Randy gave me a hug and said, "Don't worry, Deb, I can always build you a fireplace someday."

Well, "someday" turned into years, and three children later, the plans for a fireplace were forgotten. Well, not really. Things like paying the bills and feeding and clothing the kids just took priority. Money was tight for us, especially during the holidays. But there is one Christmas that I will never forget. The gifts under the tree were few; Randy and I had decided not to spend money on gifts for each other that year. Christmas Eve I spent an especially long time tucking the kids into bed. The excitement for Christmas morning always made it difficult for them to get to sleep. When I finally served the last drink of water, gave the last goodnight kiss, and prayed the last prayer, I sighed a tired sigh as I went out to the living room to join Randy with the task of last-minute gift wrapping. Instead, I entered into a softly lit room where he was sitting on a blanket. Behind him was a fireplace that he had made out of cardboard, complete with a plug-in fire log. The light from the "fire" was flickering, and my eyes were tearing up. We cuddled together in front of our fireplace, the warmest gift I have ever received.

To ensure you and your mate get a grip on the Word, picture your hand outstretched and someone handing you an important document. Immediately you would hold on to that important treasure with all five fingers. To secure the Word in your home and heart, layer the Word in five ways:

1. Hear. Attend church weekly and take notes or write key thoughts from the sermon directly next to the text in your Bible so they are there for reference later. Turn on Christian radio and TV. Purchase messages from authors or buy books on tape.

2. Read. Each day, pull out a devotional and spend 5 to 15 minutes with God. We designed our study guide for *Men Are Like Waffles—Women Are Like Spaghetti* to help couples do this together. One of our mentors, Norm Wright, wrote *Quiet Times for Couples* to help couples be in the Word together. Spending time alone with God is of equal value. That's often when God gets my attention and I hear the whisper, *The way you talked to Bill last night was unkind. Go apologize.*

One of my favorite ways to read God's Word daily is from *The Daily Bible,* which provides a format for people to read the entire Bible in a year. *Daily Light for the Daily Path* offers morning and evening readings of verses strung together by topic. We encourage people to find a Bible translation that speaks to them. A modern version like *The Message* might be best for you. Bill and I prefer NIV or NASB because they are more literal translations. The key is to find a Bible you enjoy reading and then read it daily!

3. Study. Just reading is a great thing, but you will get more out of the Word if you dig a little deeper. Even the simple practice of asking a few questions of the text will help you learn to apply it more to your life. Try this inductive method:

A. *Observation.* What does it say? Note the tone, repeated words, lists, and other simple facts about the text.

B. *Interpretation.* What does it mean? Look for cause and effect relationships, words you don't understand, and the author's main point.

C. *Application.* What does it mean to me? Construct a plan for applying the teaching to your own life.

A wonderful tool to help you study the Bible for yourself and learn these tools is the *New Inductive Study Bible* created by Kay Arthur (Harvest House Publishers).

Being in a small group Bible study where couples come together to read and discuss the Bible will impact your marriage positively. You'll hear many perspectives, you'll see how the Word is worked out in other lives, and you'll learn to apply the positive to your own. Take the initiative, invite some friends over, and begin a couples' study.

4. Memorize. When we are going through a tough time, I will use the Bible software on my computer to look up verses that address the topic we're dealing with, such as money, intimacy, or our future. I select a few to guide my prayers all day long. In this way I am also memorizing the truth so that it is available when we need it. Verses like "A gentle answer turns away wrath" and "Be quick to listen, slow to speak" often save us from having an argument. Verses like "I came that they may have life, and have it abundantly" and "I know the plans that I have for you...to give you a future and a hope" give us confidence when tough circumstances enter our lives. When the truth fills your thoughts, it counters the negative messages that daily bombard you.

5. Meditate. This is not some Eastern emptying of the mind. Meditation on God's Word means you just think about it and how it applies to your life. Ruth Graham's method of meditating on God's truth is a great example. Billy was always on the road, and she was left with a houseful of children. She longed for more time in God's Word, so she simply opened up her Bible and laid it on the kitchen counter. Whenever she walked by the Bible, she read a phrase and thought about it for a while. The Word of God "walked" into her heart and life. One way that Bill and I meditate is by listening to the Bible on CD and to verses set to music. A musical background to the truth helps the truth stick in our heads and hearts.

Share It with Others

Why do some couples seem to live happily ever after? How can you remodel your love life and turn a fixer-upper into a dream home? One key to having a happy marriage is to share with others the love that God gave you.

I (Pam) had a friend who was far from God. She had never been married but had three children, all from different dads. When I met her, she was living with a condom salesman. She had tried every spiritual practice under the sun, and her newest kick was visiting palm readers and wearing crystals for good luck. She had all kinds of questions about God, so I asked her if she wanted to learn what the Bible had to say about God.

Each week she had questions, often with ads from a New Age newspaper, such as "Jesus appearing at the Coliseum!" Yikes. We studied the uniqueness of Jesus. She heard me explain that Jesus was either a liar who died for a lie (which no sane person would do), or He was a lunatic (but then why do so many call Him a good man and a great teacher?), or He must be who He claimed to be: the Lord. We studied the attributes of God. We studied Christ's resurrection. We studied the reliability of the Bible. It was Bible school 101. Week after week, she had more questions but no life change. I was concerned for her future and the future of her children. That was what motivated me in the beginning, but I was getting a bit discouraged because nothing I said seemed to make any difference.

Then one day, after we completed our Bible study, we had planned to take the kids to the beach together. At the time, our second car was in the shop, so Bill was going to run his car home for me to take. He was running late, so he did what he always does when he runs late: He stopped and bought me flowers near where we live for just a few dollars. He walked in, gave me a kiss, said "I'm sorry," and handed me the keys and flowers.

My friend then turned to me and said, "Did your God make him do that?"

"I guess you could say that. Yes, God led Bill to do that."

"Okay, I'm ready to know your God!"

Take It from Us

In a survey we conducted, every one of the couples wrote about the need for Christ to be the center of a marriage. One couple added, "It isn't just having a common faith. The faith needs to be Christian. Women are not treated well in many religions, so marriages are not very kind or loving in many faiths. Jesus, and His example of valuing people of both genders enough to die for them, sets the foundation on which to build a loving, lasting marriage."

While at a Christian booksellers convention, I asked some national leaders with long-term marriages what advice they would give to couples. Kay Arthur, author of *A Marriage Without Regrets* and cofounder of Precept Ministries International, is passionate as she encourages couples to get into the Word. "Even if only one of you is willing to do it, the Word will positively impact the relationship!"

Jim and Elizabeth George, the authors of *A Husband After God's Own Heart* and *A Wife After God's Own Heart,* said they reminded their own newly wedded children, "Who you are at home is who you are." They stress living with kindness and integrity behind closed doors.

Becky Burke's advice was to take a fun day off each week, and her husband, Dale, the author of *Different by Design,* clarified what that meant: "Marriages would be strengthened if couples took a day off—yep, more mid-Monday-morning sex would keep the husbands happy!"

The couples we surveyed also mentioned the need to pray and attend church. They all noted that a sense of humor is imperative and that couples need to take time to talk daily, find some things they enjoy doing together, and have other activities they do individually. And make love often. Here are a few one-liners worth passing on:

About sex:

- Make love to each other regularly. Don't get into a habit of not going to bed together.
- Sex is God's greatest gift, after grace! Enjoy it! If you don't enjoy it, figure out why and fix it!
- Don't stop hugging and being romantic.

About being nice:

- Agree that you're committed to one another. Demonstrate that commitment by doing something the other person wants done.

- Study about grace so that you can both grow up and learn to forgive each other.
- Find behaviors your partner really enjoys and do those things for him or her.
- Always be loyal to your spouse and make him or her look good.
- Don't put your spouse down, and don't be sarcastic with each other.
- Don't say everything you think.

About habits that build love:

- Don't let your kids drain the life out of you or your marriage.
- Submission is real—get over it.
- God is available and wants to be the center part of your marriage.
- Learn to pray together and talk about the important things before they become big issues.
- Don't take everything personally.
- Don't try to be God for your spouse. Keep your focus on the Lord and become what He wants you to be.
- Don't pray, *"Lord, fix my mate!"* Instead, pray, *"Lord, fix me!"*
- Don't go to bed angry. You'll just wake up angry the next morning.
- Seek supportive friendships with other couples.
- Go to counseling, and try to talk out your problems as much as possible ahead of time.
- Turn off the TV.

One couple who are edging up on 40 years together say, "In our opinion, any marriage that has these two things going for it can succeed:

1. Learn to speak the truth in love to each other.
2. Look out for the other's interests before your own.

As married couples, our instructions are clear. We should each seek to be like Christ:

> If you have any encouragement from being united with Christ, if any comfort from his love, if any fellowship with the Spirit, if any tenderness and compassion, then make my joy complete by being like-minded, having the same love, being one in spirit and purpose. Do nothing out of selfish ambition or vain conceit, but in humility consider others better than yourselves. Each of you should look not only to your own interests, but also to the interests of others. Your attitude should be the same as that of Christ Jesus: Who, being in very nature God, did not consider equality with God something to be grasped, but made himself nothing, taking the very nature of a servant (Philippians 2:1-7).

The Payoff

We have been called many things: Reverend and Mrs. Farrel, Mom and Dad, Bill and Pam. But when Bill whispers, "Angel," I melt. One night, I was struck with the realization that our love is an amazing gift. I put pen to paper and wrote a poem to Bill to express how speechless he made me feel when he loved me with God's powerful, protective, providing love:

> Beyond words
> or phrases
> or prose penned,
> Beyond the lines and meter

and rhythm
and rhyme,
Beyond a syllable whispered
or sound released...
Language cannot reach
the place where your love
has carried me.

An elderly couple sat on their porch rocking back and forth looking at the sunset on their sixtieth anniversary. The husband looked at his wife and asked, "Darling, whatever happened to our sexual relations?"

She thought a while and replied, "I'm not certain, dear. They didn't even send us a card last Christmas."

Mentor Moments

Have you been married a long time? Has God given you some wisdom you could share? Consider inviting a younger couple out for lunch once a week or once a month to talk about a chapter from *The 10 Best Decisions a Couple Can Make.* You could use 1 Corinthians 13:4-8,13 as your key verses. The questions and ideas below can help you get your discussion started.

Chapter 1—Decide to Build a Love That Lasts

1. What has been your biggest surprise in marriage?
2. What would you like your marriage to be like five or ten years from now?

Chapter 2—Decide to Be Positive

1. Have you experienced an emotional disaster in your marriage? What issue caused it?
2. What helped you recover?
3. What have you learned from the experience that you could apply in a similar situation?

Chapter 3—Decide to Communicate with Kindness

1. In what ways do you already communicate with kindness?
2. Share one thing about communication you learned from this chapter.
3. What is one thing from the chapter you would like to begin or become more consistent doing?

Chapter 4—Decide to Fight Fair

1. What is your conflict resolution style?

2. What would you like to change about the way you handle a disagreement?

Chapter 5—Decide "We" Is Greater than "Me"

1. What do you most value and appreciate about your family of origin?

2. What family values or habits have you changed (or do you need to change)?

3. Does anything from your past continue to be a negative influence?

4. When does it usually become an issue?

5. Brainstorm some other ways to handle the negative feelings or behaviors.

Chapter 6—Decide to Keep the Sex Sizzling

1. Describe the most romantic date you've ever enjoyed.

2. What first attracted you to your mate?

3. What has been the happiest day in your marriage since your wedding?

4. Share your favorite romantic spots in your city.

Chapter 7—Decide to Discover Your Spouse's Life Motivation

1. What did you learn about your mate as you read this chapter?

2. Describe one characteristic of your spouse's personality that you appreciate and that is opposite from your personality. Why do you appreciate this characteristic?

Chapter 8—Decide to Tackle Transitions

1. Describe the life stage or transition you are experiencing right now.

2. What changes will the next few years probably bring?

3. What can you do to prepare for the road ahead?

4. What has been your hardest transition so far?

5. How would you advise others to handle this difficult transition in a way that will strengthen their marriage?

   (Bring your marriage mission statement and your family crest to your next meeting.)

Chapter 9—Decide to Leave a Legacy of Love

1. Share your marriage mission statement and the meaning of your crest.

2. What legacy would you like for your marriage to leave?

3. What family traditions have you established (or would you like to start) that will inspire your children and grandchildren to build a long-lasting love?

Chapter 10—Decide to Connect to the Author of Love

1. How have you recently used any of the five tools for getting a firm grip on the Word (hear, read, study, memorize, meditate)? How would you like to begin using one?

2. Are you ministering or volunteering as a couple? If not, can you think of a way you would like to begin?

3. Every couple has a love story. Whom can you share your love story with?

Now that you have finished discussing *The 10 Best Decisions a Couple Can Make,* set a time and place to enjoy a double date together!

Group Discussion Questions

In each of the chapters below, the group discussion questions are followed by a special date-night discussion starter. Make time as a couple each week to enjoy a walk, a dinner out, a car ride, or some other activity that will give you 20 to 60 minutes of time without the kids to emotionally connect. Connecting emotionally may entice you to stretch the time and connect physically as well!

Chapter 1—Decide to Build a Love That Lasts

1. How would a Realtor describe your marriage? (Cozy and quiet bungalow in a safe neighborhood? Adventurous cabin in the wilderness? High-rise with a great view?) Write a two-line real estate ad and use it to introduce yourself and your spouse to the group.

2. What has been your biggest surprise in marriage so far?

3. The key verses that this book is based on are 1 Corinthians 13:4-8,13. Which trait of love is easiest for you to live out? Which is the most difficult?

4. What does each of the verses below teach you about building a love that lasts?

   • Romans 14:19

   • 1 Corinthians 3:10

   • 1 Corinthians 3:11-13

Date-night discussion starter: What dreams do you have for your marriage? Describe what you would like your marriage to be like five years from now.

Chapter 2—Decide to Be Positive

1. This chapter includes 11 ideas for recovering from an emotional disaster. Which is the most natural for you as a couple? Which is new to you?

2. What has your experience taught you about recovering from an emotional disaster?

3. What have you learned from the first two chapters that has helped strengthen your relationship?

4. Marriage requires a lot of patience because we are imperfect people. Read each verse that follows, restate it in your own words, and share how you could apply it to your marriage.

   • Galatians 5:22-23

   • Ephesians 4:1-3

   • 1 Thessalonians 5:14

   • 2 Timothy 2:24

5. On pages 32–33, Phil Callaway lists five reasons he and Ramona have enjoyed a long-lasting marriage. What did you learn from him that you want to apply to your own life?

6. What circumstances are likely to make you impatient? What habits or choices help you to be patient?

7. How can a stronger relationship with God help you be more patient?

8. What has been the hardest issue for you as a couple? What was the secret to your success?

9. Take turns praying for each other, asking that each person will experience God-empowered patience this week.

   Date-night discussion starter: Describe a time when your spouse was extremely patient with you. Thank him or her and share how his or her patience made you feel.

Chapter 3—Decide to Communicate with Kindness

1. What is the best trait of your relationship?

2. What tool from the garage most resembles the way you typically communicate or handle conflict? Share why you chose that tool.

3. Pam and Bill share about a miscommunication they had. Describe a humorous (or not so humorous) miscommunication you've had as a couple. How did you solve the misunderstanding?

4. Review this checklist from the chapter:

   • Check the timing.

   • Check the closeness.

   • Check the tone of voice, body language, and attitude.

   • Check in with God.

   Which one of these items will you work on this week? Why did you choose that item?

5. Read 2 Peter 1:4-8. Kindness is on the list of several things God wants for us. Define these terms in your own words and share how each can strengthen a marriage:

   • diligence　　　　　　• self control

   • moral excellence　　• perseverance

   • knowledge　　　　　• godliness

6. Review the "Verizon plan":

   • Move location (get a better perspective).

   • Call back (avoid static).

   • Call the operator (get help).

   Which communication tool would you like to begin using or learn to use more effectively?

   Date-night discussion starter: The end of the chapter includes a list of kind, affirming words, such as "I love you," "I appreciate you," and "We're a good team." Write a letter affirming your mate. List his or her good qualities and strengths, and note the things that attracted you to him or her. Read it aloud at dinner. What was the kindest thing your spouse ever said to you? How did that make you feel? Can you remember other kind words your spouse has given you?

Chapter 4—Decide to Fight Fair

1. The thing you love about your mate can become a source of irritation. Turn the coin over and remember what first attracted you to him or her. Introduce your spouse to the group the way you would have when you first met.

2. Review this list of conflict resolution styles. Which describes you?

   - negotiator
   - debater
   - peacekeeper
   - drama team
   - survivor
   - servant

3. Envy and jealousy are sinful cousins. See if you can come up with a definition for each. Here are some verses that will help:

   - Job 5:2
   - Proverbs 3:31; 6:34; 14:30
   - Proverbs 23:17; 27:4
   - Ecclesiastes 4:4
   - Song of Solomon 8:6
   - Ezekiel 35:11
   - Nahum 1:2
   - Acts 13:45
   - 1 Corinthians 3:3
   - Galatians 5:19-21

4. How can envy or jealousy cause conflict in a marriage?

   Date-night discussion starter: Begin by complimenting your spouse by recalling one time he or she handled a disagreement or difference of opinion well. Then identify one thing you would like to change about the way you handle a disagreement.

Chapter 5—Decide "We" Is Greater than "Me"

1. Recall a time that your mate gave up something for you.

2. What are the results of working on your marriage as a team? What are the results when each of you try to protect your own interests?

3. Pride kills love. Egocentric living and narcissistic actions are common today. Can you think of couples in the headlines that express this selfish behavior?

4. Read Isaiah 14:10-23. Pride goes all the way back to the beginning of time. God created Lucifer as a wonderful, beautiful angel who would lead the worship of God. But Satan decided he should be worshipped. He felt he was as good as God—the epitome of pride. How does pride creep into a marriage?

5. Read these verses and list some of the results of pride:

   • Psalm 73:6

   • Proverbs 11:2; 16:18; 29:23

   • 1 John 2:16-17

6. Think of a person you know who is prideful. What are other people's reactions to someone who is proud and boastful?

7. Bill describes sky hooks as imaginary statements we want to be true—but are not. What kind of lame excuses or made-up relationship rules are common today? Here's one example:

   • Sky hook: Whoever yells the loudest wins the argument.

   • The truth: Yelling never solves anything!

8. Read John 8:32 and Romans 12:1-2. What does God say will make our relationships work?

Date-night discussion starters:

1. What strengths do you love most about the family you came from? What weaknesses have you overcome?

2. Do any negative habits from your past creep into your present? What issues or situations trigger those negative habits? How might you handle those issues or situations more effectively?

Chapter 6—Decide to Keep the Sex Sizzling

1. What are a couple of your favorite romantic spots in your city?

2. Describe the most romantic date you've ever enjoyed.

3. What has been the happiest day in your marriage since your wedding?

4. What first attracted you to your mate?

5. The backdrop to a sizzling sex life is to be selfless—focused on your mate and not yourself. Read Philippians 2:3-5. Make your own list of five to ten character traits and attributes of Christ that you can emulate. How can each trait make you a better spouse, a better lover, or a better friend to your mate?

6. Compliment your mate in front of the group. When has he or she been most Christlike? What is the most selfless act he or she ever did on your behalf?

7. When is it hardest for you to be selfless? What helps you change your attitude and begin to focus on others again?

   Date-night idea: Set a date this week where you each make the other the top priority from the time you see each other after work until you go to sleep. You may want to take requests behind closed bedroom doors so that each of you can love your spouse in his or her favorite ways. Give each other the three gifts mentioned in the chapter:

   • Admiration: Compliment your mate from head to toe.

   • Anticipation: Call, write, e-mail, or give a gift that says "I look forward to being with you."

   • Adventure: Ask your spouse, "What would you like to try?"

Chapter 7—Decide to Discover Your Spouse's Life Motivation

1. Describe one characteristic of your spouse's personality that you appreciate and that is opposite from your personality. Why do you appreciate this characteristic?

2. Read Proverbs 22:6; Psalm 139:13; Jeremiah 1:5. What do these verses tell us about the way God creates us?

3. What tool commonly found in a toolbox or garage describes your mate? (Be complimentary!)

4. Review your personal motivational tools:

   - personality style
   - conflict resolution style
   - learning style
   - love language
   - birth order
   - relax and recharge style
   - spiritual gift
   - financial style
   - parenting style

   What have you learned about yourself this week? What have you learned about your mate?

5. What is the benefit of knowing the strengths of each person in your family? How can knowing this information about your spouse strengthen your marriage?

Date-night discussion starters:

1. What did you learn about yourself this week that your spouse should know?

2. What is one of your strengths that you can share more with your family?

3. Compliment your spouse on one of his or her strengths.

Chapter 8—Decide to Tackle Transitions

1. Read Ecclesiastes 3. There is a time for every event under heaven. What life stage or transition are you in now?

2. What life stage or transition will you be likely to experience in the next few years?

3. What can you do to prepare for the road ahead?

4. What has been your hardest transition so far?

5. How would you encourage younger couples to handle that transition in a way that brings them closer together?

6. Has a particular Bible verse given you strength in the tough seasons of life? Share it with the group.

   (Bring your marriage mission statement and your family crest to next week's meeting.)

   Date-night discussion starter: What might be on the road ahead in the next five years? Create a plan that will help you successfully navigate your next life transitions.

Chapter 9—Decide to Leave a Legacy of Love

1. What word or symbol best describes your marriage?

2. Read Psalm 33:11; 45:17; 71:18; 145:4. What truths are we to pass down from generation to generation?

3. Share your marriage mission statement and your family crest with the group. What is the legacy you want your marriage to leave?

4. What family traditions have you established that will inspire your children and grandchildren to build a long-lasting love?

Date-night discussion starters:

1. What family traditions would you like to begin that will empower your children to value marriage and family?

2. What family traditions can make your love shine as a light of the gospel?

Chapter 10—Decide to Connect to the Author of Love

1. Whom do you know that would benefit the most from hearing your love story?

2. Read 1 John 4:15-16 and 1 Corinthians 13:7-8. When you put these two Scriptures together, what do you learn about God?

3. How has God protected your marriage? How has He helped you to develop trust?

4. Describe a situation when God really came through for you as a couple.

5. What do these verses teach you about persevering under stress?

   - Matthew 6:31-34
   - Matthew 11:28-30
   - Romans 8:37-38
   - 1 Corinthians 10:13
   - 2 Corinthians 1:3-4
   - Philippians 4:6-7
   - 1 Peter 1:6-7
   - 1 Peter 5:7,10

6. In giving we gain as a couple. How has serving God enriched your relationship through giving?

7. What new ministry or volunteer service could you participate in as a couple?

   Date-night idea: Celebrate the end of this ten-week study as a group with a dinner party. Have each couple invite another couple who is new to the area, new to church, new in relationship with God, or not yet in a relationship with Christ. At the party, take turns sharing your love stories, and include at least one verse or reference to Christ. Get the word out that God is love!

Notes

Chapter 2—Decide to Be Positive

1. Phil Callaway, "I Proposed in a Chain Letter," *Marriage Partnership,* Spring 2003, p. 52.

Chapter 4—Decide to Fight Fair

1. Clayton Tucker-Ladd, "Dating, Love, Marriage, and Sex," *Psychological Self-Help,* www.psychologicalselfhelp.org/chapter10/chapter10_51.html.

2. Debra White Smith, *Romancing Your Husband* (Eugene, OR: Harvest House Publishers, 2002).

Chapter 6—Decide to Keep the Sex Sizzling

1. C.F. Kiel and F. Delitch, *Commentary on the Old Testament,* vol. 6 (Grand Rapids: Eerdmans Publishing Company, 1978), p. 72.

2. Joseph Dillow, *Solomon on Sex* (Nashville: Thomas Nelson, 1977), p. 77.

3. Tim LaHaye, *How to Be Happy Though Married* (Wheaton, IL: Tyndale House Publishers, 1968), p. 64.

4. Dillow, *Solomon on Sex,* p. 114.

Chapter 8—Decide to Tackle Transitions

1. www.marriage-relationships.com/divorce_statistics.html.

2. www.smartmarriages.com/before.breakup.html.

3. Scott M. Stanley and Howard J. Markman, "Acting on What We Know," www.smartmarriages.com/hope.html.

4. Willliam Doherty, "Intentional Marriage: Your Rituals Will Set You Free," www.smartmarriages.com/intentionalmarriage.html.

5. Ibid.

6. Brenda Hunter, *Where Have All the Mothers Gone?* (Grand Rapids: Zondervan, 1982), p. 90.

7. www.divorcemag.com/statistics/statsUS.shtml.

8. www.marriage-relationships.com/divorce_statistics.html.

9. See www.wivesinprayer.org and www.seasonedsisters.com.

10. See www.rand.org/pubs/research_briefs/RB5030/index1.html.

11. Mike McManus, "Giving 'Marriage Insurance' to the Engaged," www.smartmarriages.com/mentor.mcmanus.html.

12. For similar research, see Richard B. Miller, "Do Children Make a Marriage Unhappy?" at marriageandfamilies.byu.edu/issues/2001/April/children.aspx.

Chapter 9—Decide to Leave a Legacy of Love

1. Helen Duff Baugh, *The Story Goes On* (Kansas City, MO: Stonecroft Ministries, 1984), p. 15.

2. www.cbcc.net/history.htm.

Chapter 10—Decide to Connect to the Author of Love

1. *Our Daily Bread*, February 14, 1993.

For more resources to enhance your relationships
and build marriages or to connect with
Bill and Pam Farrel for a speaking engagement, contact

Farrel Communications
Masterful Living Ministries
3755 Avocado Blvd., #414
La Mesa, CA 91941
800-810-4449

farrelcommunications.com
www.masterfulliving.com

For help with marriage issues in midlife, visit
www.seasonedsisters.com

Other Great Harvest House Books by the Farrels

MEN ARE LIKE WAFFLES—WOMEN ARE LIKE SPAGHETTI
Men keep life elements in separate boxes; women intertwine everything. Providing biblical insights, sound research, and humorous anecdotes, the Farrels explore gender differences and preferences and how they can strengthen relationships.

THE 10 BEST DECISIONS A WOMAN CAN MAKE
Bestselling author Pam Farrel encourages you to exchange the fleeting standards of the world for the steadfast truths found in a growing, fruitful relationship with God as you find your place in His plan.

THE 10 BEST DECISIONS EVERY PARENT CAN MAKE
With biblical insight and personal experience, the Farrels encourage you to make the ten most important decisions that will nurture and celebrate strong-willed, prodigal, and special-needs kids.

RED-HOT MONOGAMY
With their trademark insight, humor, and candid personal perspectives, Bill and Pam Farrel reveal the truths about the sexual relationship in marriage and what husbands and wives need to know to keep the embers burning.

FANTASTIC AFTER 40
Pam Farrel shares words of encouragement, challenge, and humor to give you the inspiration you long for. Designed for personal or group study, this empowering read gives life-enhancing resources to forge a fulfilling future and maximize midlife and beyond.

HARVEST HOUSE
PUBLISHERS

CPSIA information can be obtained at www.ICGtesting.com
Printed in the USA
LVOW05s0106071014

407465LV00016BA/823/P